Jackie Sproul

★ REFLECTIONS OF A ★
BLACK COWBOY

BOOK THREE ★ PIONEERS

★ REFLECTIONS OF A ★
BLACK COWBOY

BY ROBERT H. MILLER

ILLUSTRATED BY RICHARD LEONARD

SILVER BURDETT PRESS

Copyright © 1991 by Robert Miller
Illustrations © 1991 by Richard Leonard
All rights reserved including the right of reproduction in whole or in part in
any form.
Published by Silver Burdett Press, Inc., a division of Simon & Schuster, Inc.,
Prentice Hall Bldg., Englewood Cliffs, NJ 07632.
Designed by Leslie Bauman
Manufactured in the United States of America
10 9 8 7 6

Library of Congress Cataloging-in-Publication Data
Miller, Robert H. (Robert Henry)
Reflections of a Black cowboy.
Includes bibliographical references (p. 101)
Contents: bk. 1. Cowboys—bk. 3. Pioneers
1. Afro-American cowboys—West (U.S.)—Biography—Juvenile literature.   2.
West (U.S.)—Biography—Juvenile literature.   3. West (U.S.)—Social life and
customs—Juvenile literature. [1. Cowboys.   2. Afro-Americans—Biography.
3. West (U.S.)—Biography.]   I. Title.
P596.M646   1991
978' .00496073022
[B]   91-8661
ISBN 0-382-24081-2 (lib. bdg.) ISBN 0-382-24086-3 (pbk.)

CONTENTS

PREFACE

Welcome to *Reflections of a Black Cowboy*. The books in this series were written to introduce you, the reader, to African-American people who helped settle the West. You'll meet cowboys, pioneers, soldiers, scouts, and mail drivers, and be part of history as our narrator the Old Cowboy remembers some stories from days gone by.

As young boys, my brother John and I would sit on the floor around my mother's favorite chair, waiting quietly for her to read us a story. She liked to read to us about faraway places and magical times. When I closed my eyes, I could see myself in the story—as a bystander or one of the main characters or often as the hero.

Like many black children growing up in the fifties, my heroes were drawn from the movies. Many of my favorite movies were westerns. Judging from what I saw in these movies, I figured there were no black cowboys. In the movies, most blacks had roles in the background as cooks or shoeshine boys or stable hands. Unfortunately, those weren't exactly the roles I had in mind for myself when I strapped on my play gun and holster outfit.

It was after one of those games of Cowboys and Indians that my mother told John and me a few new stories about her uncles, Ed and Joe Cloud. We thought "Cloud" was a strange-sounding name. Our mother explained that our great uncles were cowboys who had traveled throughout Texas and Mexico. Often, they had to shoot their way out of trouble on cattle drives.

From that day on, John and I had a different perspective when we played our games of Cowboys and Indians. Instead of Hollywood movie stars, our uncles became our heroes.

This book is an effort to help define our cultural heritage and to pay tribute to Ed and Joe Cloud and all the other black men and women who helped tame the West.

Journey back with me now to that place called the wild, wild West, where you can be whoever *you* want. All you need is a fast horse, some boots, and a saddle. Now close your eyes—enjoy the ride!

Robert Miller

INTRODUCTION

The word "pioneer" refers to someone who breaks new ground and paves new paths for others to follow. This is certainly true for African Americans who went West during the nineteenth century. Spurred on by tales of freedom or intoxicated with a sense of adventure, African Americans escaped slavery in the South for the quest of new horizons on the western frontier.

The man known as York was one of those pioneers. Born into slavery in Virginia, York was a childhood friend of William Clark, one of the leaders of the famed Lewis and Clark expedition. York accompanied Clark on the dangerous journey through Indian country in the West and served with such intelligence and bravery that Clark freed him on their return to the Mississippi. Raucous Ed "Cut Nose" Rose, a great hunter and fur trapper who helped build the fortunes of John Jacob Astor, one of America's first millionaires, blazed his way into western history, too. The feats of these African-American adventurers became legendary as old-timers spun tales about them around many a campside fire.

Mining, especially gold mining, drew many pioneers out West. Alvin Coffey, an African American who worked hard in the mining camps, was one of those men. He eventually bought his freedom through his own labor and persistence. African-American women, too, heeded the call of the West. If ever there was a pioneer who pointed out the meaning of "true grit," it was Biddy Mason. She herded sheep for her master and walked from Mississippi to California behind three hundred ox-drawn wagon trains. Arriving in California, a state where slavery was outlawed, she sued for her freedom and the freedom of her three daughters and won. In time, Biddy became one of California's most wealthy and respected businesswomen and landowners. Pony Express riders, such as George Monroe, also played a role in opening up the West. Before the telegraph spanned the nation, Monroe and African Americans like him galloped at break-neck speed from station to station to carry mail and parcels from east to west and back again.

These are but a few of the memories of the West that time and many history books have forgotten. By opening these doors to the past, we can learn more about ourselves and our nation. So pull up a chair, relax, and enjoy a ride back to the very early days of the "black pioneers."

A SURPRISE VISITOR

Late in the afternoon an old man known as the Old Cowboy and his dog, Sundown, struggled up a trail as they made their way into the high country of the Rocky Mountains. A chill wind that sounded like a lonesome freight train whistle blew down the mountain passes and made the Old Cowboy pull his sheepskin duster closer to his body.

It was elk season again in Colorado. The Old Cowboy loved to hunt elk, and he didn't mind traveling from Montana to Colorado each year to test his talents as a "master hunter," a name the Indians gave him a long time ago. The Indians had a lot of respect for the Old Cowboy. See, the Old Cowboy was a black man, and they figured he had been through some of the same hard times as they had. Well, the Old Cowboy reckoned he had seen some rough times. But he had lived through a few good spells, too. He had met an awful lot of wranglers, gunfighters, and mountain men during his years, and he had a mind to tell Sundown about a few of these characters, just as soon as they got to where they were going.

"We better hurry up, Sundown. Looks like Old Man Winter 'bout to put on his walking shoes," he said, slapping his horse into a fast gallop. They had been on the road for some time, and waiting just around the bend was the hunting cabin he'd built many years ago. Barking and running far out in front, Sundown pranced down the road. He knew this part of Colorado as well as the Old Cowboy and sensed that they had almost reached their destination. The sky was fiery red when the Old Cowboy and Sundown rode up and stopped a few yards from the cabin.

"Sundown, hold up, boy!" the Old Cowboy shouted, dismounting his horse as though he expected danger. They had been away a whole year. Anything could be inside that old cabin.

Once, in a situation like this, he and Sundown had been surprised by a grizzly bear that was almost as big as a locomotive. It had been touch and go for awhile, until Sundown had grabbed hold of that grizzly's nose with his fangs. The Old Cowboy didn't intend to get bushwacked by a grizzly or a mountain lion or a wolverine ever again. He motioned for Sundown to be careful.

Following his master's orders, Sundown carefully circled around back of the cabin. The two of them were like a team. They had been together so long you'd think they had the same mind. Like a mountain lion creeping up to an unsuspecting doe, the Old Cowboy slowly tiptoed to the blind side of the

cabin, carbine rifle at the ready. You never knew what to expect after being away for a year. A man's survival in the wild depended on him being aware of everything—even those animal tracks he noticed along the road that led straight to the cabin. At first, he figured they were óld and dismissed them, but when he saw the door slightly opened he shouted for Sundown to hold up. Crawling like a baby on his hands and knees, he silently ducked under the front window so he couldn't be seen and inched his way to the front door.

Sundown was in the back waiting for his master's signal. They had played this game many a time. Even though the back door was slightly ajar, he wouldn't enter until the Old Cowboy gave the signal. Holding his breath until the very last minute, the Old Cowboy eased his hand across the wooden splinters of the old front door until he gripped the very edge. In one quick motion, he swung open the door and pointing his carbine straight ahead, gave a "coyote yell" that would have grown hair on a rock. Sundown sliced through the opening in the back door like a bolt of lightning, and, boy, did they have a surprise waiting for them. Chewing on a worn out tablecloth was a lost baby mountain goat, looking just as surprised at all the commotion as they were. The Old Cowboy fell down on his knees and started laughing so hard he nearly rolled off the front porch. Sundown stopped dead in his tracks when he saw the baby goat. You'd have thought he'd been sprayed in the face by a skunk.

When he had recovered from his shock, the Old Cowboy entered the cabin.

"So you're the varmint causing all the ruckus," he said. "I bet you must be mighty hungry to be eating up my only tablecloth. Let's get you some real food, little fella."

He patted the baby goat softly on the head, then disappeared out the door. A moment later, he came back with

some grub he had packed in his saddlebag and fed the baby goat while Sundown, licking his chops and glancing up every now and then, tried to catch his master's eye.

"You trying to tell me something?" the Old Cowboy asked. "I'll be with you in a minute." Turning his attention back to the baby goat, he said, "Your mama is probably looking for you right this minute. Come on with me."

He led the baby goat outside. "Now that your belly's full, you best be hitting the road," he said.

It was just about dark when the Old Cowboy put the baby goat outside. The little goat looked puzzled. He didn't know which way to go, so he turned and stared the Old Cowboy in the face with those big, baby goat eyes that begged to stay.

"Looks like we got ourselves some company tonight, Sundown!"

For the first time that night, Sundown had a stranger sharing his dinner. The Old Cowboy made a fire and lit his favorite pipe.

Sundown just looked up from his usual position, laying at the feet of the Old Cowboy, and yawned. He was about to go to sleep. The baby goat rested quietly on its haunches, trying desperately to keep awake.

"You two ain't gonna go to sleep on me yet. No sir, not until I tell both of you a few of my favorite stories. And you little fella," the Old Cowboy said, talking to the baby goat, "I'm puttin' you out first thing in the morning. I know your mama is wondering where you are. Now let's see, which story will I tell tonight . . ." He pulled his chin as he thought. "Oh, yes . . . being snuggled up in these mountains reminds me of a fella who tramped these parts before. He was a tough cuss, that's for sure—toughest, straightest-shooting fella this side of Cheyenne . . ."

YORK AND THE LEWIS AND CLARK EXPEDITION

"You know, Sundown, I've traveled all over this country. Of course, I spent most of my time in the West. But before the West opened up to white settlers, it was all wilderness. See, the United States only claimed land east of the Mississippi River; all land west of the Mississippi was owned by France and Spain.

"In 1804, President Thomas Jefferson paid money to buy Louisiana and a good chunk of land that lay west of the Mississippi River from a fellow named Napoleon, who was the emperor of France. This jumbo-sized piece of real estate was called the Louisiana Purchase and eventually would hold the states of Louisiana, Arkansas, Oklahoma, Missouri, Iowa, Kansas, Ne-

braska, Minnesota, North and South Dakota, part of Colorado, Wyoming, and Montana.

"You see, Sundown, nobody knew much about what lay in this wilderness. To find out what was out there, President Jefferson commissioned a grand expedition to go out and explore the country. This journey was called the Lewis and Clark expedition after the two leaders of the venture, Meriwether Lewis and William Clark. Now, all this is a well-known part of the history of our country. But what is not so well known is the story of a black man named York who also went along.

Word had it that York was born about 1770 as the house slave to the Clark family in Virginia. He ran around the plantation and got to be very friendly with their young son, William Clark. Both boys were the same age and Mr. Clark didn't see no harm in William having a playmate so long as York understood his place.

"Hush now," whispered York as he and William crept up slowly on the raccoon. It was a warm summer day on the plantation and little York and William were having some fun playing with a mother raccoon and her babies. "You got to be quiet else they run off if they hear you," said York. Messing with a mother raccoon and her babies can be trouble, as the two ten-year-old fellows soon found out. York had just gotten close enough to grab one of the baby raccoons when the mother turned around and sprayed him and William right in the face.

"Ohhh!" yelled William. As he tried to get away, he tripped over York, who fell down and rolled on the ground, trying to get the raccoon smell off his face and body.

"Last one to the pond stinks!" shouted William. Both

boys raced for the pond and jumped in, laughing and splashing water on one another.

''How many times I told you to stop chasing after them skunks. You smell to high heaven,'' scolded York's mother. ''You and the master's boy gon' get yourself hurt running wild in them woods. If it ain't raccoons it's snakes. You better learn to do something 'sides play all the time.''

Young York didn't pay his mother much mind. He and William Clark were always together and liked to stay in permanent trouble.

''Son, I don't mind you playing with York, but you must understand he's a slave, and they have duties around here. I don't want you to get too close, so you think he's your equal. He's just a slave, you understand?'' said an ailing Mr. Clark.

''Yes father, I understand, but York is different. He's very smart and fun to be with. We do so many things together. I bet if he could learn to read and write like me, he'd be just as smart,'' said a proud little William Clark, who at that age didn't see any difference between the two of them.

''That, my son, will never be. He's a slave, and you're his master. He can never be as smart as you. Never! Now, no more talk about this. I want you to start spending more time with some of your other friends, your white friends. You'll be taking over this plantation someday, maybe sooner than you think if my health doesn't improve. You have to learn how to manage these slaves correctly. Now get cleaned up . . . What is that godawful smell?''

''We got squirted by a skunk; then we jumped in the pond,'' smiled William.

"We? We who?" said Mr. Clark.

"Me and York," replied his son as he took off running for his bath.

Two weeks later on a summer night, as the crickets were chirping their favorite song, William and York sat on the corral fence.

"Where you been? I ain't seen hide nor hair of you lately," said York.

"My pa had me running a lot of errands for him," William said, staring off into the night.

"I be busy myself. There's a lot of work around here," replied York.

Both young boys knew there was something they had to say but neither one wanted to say it.

"Your Pappy talk to you 'bout me?" asked York.

"Yeah, I'm not supposed to see you anymore."

"Cause I be a slave and you be the master?" York asked.

"It ain't right, my pappy said, for us to be the same. I told him you could be as smart as me if you learn to read, but that made him mad, so we can't see each other like we used to."

"We can't go huntin' bullfrogs no more?" asked York.

"Well, maybe one more time," said William, peeking over his shoulder to see if anybody heard him.

Not long after that, the Clark family and its slaves moved to Kentucky, and Mr. Clark sent young William away for more schooling. I ain't too clear where he went, but he was gone for a long time. In 1799, young William came back to help his father run the plantation in Kentucky, which was called Mulberry Hill. The older Clark was still ailing. One day Mr. Clark couldn't get out of bed, and he sent word for his son to come to him. William ran into the bedroom where his father lay. The old man looked 'bout as lifeless as the fallen leaf of a maple tree.

"Son, all my life I've worked to build this place up so that some day I could turn it over to you. Everything's in order now, but I want you to remember what I told you about the slaves. Keep them in line, even York. He's proved to be loyal but you still have to control him."

William nodded. "Yes father."

"I want to be buried next to your mother, you know that . . ." Mr. Clark mumbled. Then, unable to talk anymore, he lay still on the bed. Later that night, he died.

William Clark became boss of the plantation. He resembled a younger version of his father now. Like his father, he was short and rather ordinary looking. York, on the other hand, had sprung up into a full-grown man. He stood well over six feet tall, with muscles that bulged when he walked.

The two young men were the same age, but they had begun to grow apart. Since he had been away, William's attitudes toward black folks had begun to change. There was a different tone in his voice now, and he didn't spend much time with York. York, like many of the slaves who were friendly with masters' children when they were little, knew that one day this friendship would end. So, in a way, York wasn't surprised by what happened after the master's death. By now York and William each knew their station in life. Neither one tried to change it.

William and York worked the plantation in Kentucky for another few years. But gradually William Clark became more interested in politics and exploration than tending to his farm. You see, Clark's older brother, George, had become a general and war hero because of his campaigns against Indians in Ohio. Not one to be outdone by his own kin, William itched for a chance to sink his teeth into the virgin territory out West. He served in the Kentucky militia for awhile, but resigned in 1796. By 1804, his chance came along through his old friend Meriwether Lewis. Lewis, who was now secretary to President Jefferson, was summoned one day to the president's office.

"Mr. Lewis," the president said, "you're undoubtedly aware of that large stretch of land west of the Mississippi that I just purchased from Napoleon."

"Yes, I am, Mr. President," answered Meriwether Lewis.

"Our government needs to know more about what's out there. I understand you have been speaking to friends of yours about getting out and doing something meaningful. I know you volunteered for that failed expedition to the Pacific Northwest some years ago. How would you like to put together an exploring party and report back to me about what lies in the Louisiana Purchase?"

Lewis had been itching to get out of the White House; this was the chance he'd been waiting for. "I would consider it an honor, Mr. President. I am ready to go!" declared a cheerful Mr. Lewis.

"I must caution you, Lewis. Choose whomever you want to assist you, but remember we need to establish good relations with the Indians. Their cooperation will be important to the development of the area."

"Yes, sir, I totally agree," said Lewis.

Meriwether Lewis and William Clark had developed a friendship during their days in the Kentucky militia, and they kept in close touch with each other when Clark returned to Mulberry Hill.

That night, at one of the president's balls, Lewis sought out his friend. When Clark walked in, Lewis pulled him aside. "I've got something to tell you," he said excitedly.

"Can't it wait? I just got here," Clark replied.

"You know that land the president bought from Napoleon?"

"Yes, so what?" Clark replied.

"He wants me to start up an expedition to go out there and explore it."

"And . . ." replied Clark.

"I want you to go with me. It'll be you and me, charting unknown country."

William Clark thought about it. He, like Lewis, always loved an adventure.

"Well, don't keep me waiting. You in or out?" demanded Lewis.

Clark pretended to hesitate while he considered Lewis's proposition. Finally, he said: "Okay, I'm in, on one condition—that York comes with us. He's big, strong, and this is something he'd take to like a fish to water. Besides he might come in handy. We don't know what's out there. The more protection we have the better."

"Whatever you want. If you want to bring your favorite slave, bring him along. But if he gets in the way, he's your responsibility," said Lewis.

Both young men were as happy as roosters in a barnyard full of hens. William couldn't wait to tell York.

That moment came early one morning when York was hitching up the horses to do the plowing.

"York, come on over here. I got something I want to ask you," William said.

"Yes, sir," said York curiously.

"You been with our family a long time. We've been friends since childhood. I know things have changed between us. Well . . ."

"I ain't got no ill feelin' 'gainst you," said York.

"That's good," William Clark said, "cause I got something I want to ask you. You don't have to say yes if you don't want to, but what I want to know is . . . How would you like to go West with me to a place where no white man—or black man—has ever been before?"

"What kind of place is it?" asked York.

"That's it. Nobody knows what's there. The president bought this large piece of land and we're going out there to see what it looks like. I want you to come with me. It'll be like old times, remember?"

York did remember. They had some wild times running around like young colts, getting in all kinds of trouble.

"That sounds nice, mighty nice," York said. "When do we go?"

"We leave for St. Louis in two weeks."

"Why St. Louis?"

"We're going to train there for the trip. I'm sure glad you are coming," said a happy William Clark.

The Lewis and Clark group set up camp near St. Louis in the winter of 1804. All forty-three men carried everything they needed for their long journey. While in St. Louis, the men got in shape and learned how to take care of themselves in the wilderness. They learned how to make maps of the land and how to speak the local language.

William Clark discovered that York easily learned a lot of French and Indian words. York was busting out with pride. Here he was speaking two languages other than his natural tongue, something not even William Clark could do.

"We have to find ourselves a guide if this expedition is going to be successful," Lewis said to Clark one day.

"Where do we begin to look?" Clark replied.

"We need someone who speaks the Indian language to be able to help us communicate," Lewis said.

"You know, York has been getting along well with these Indians. Maybe he knows enough to ask around for us," Clark replied. York had been mixing well with the Shoshone Indians and had picked up enough of their language to get by. Later that afternoon, Clark stopped York.

"York we need a guide who knows this part of the country. See if you can ask around and find one for us," said Clark.

"I met an Indian woman who's very friendly. Maybe she might help us," said York. He quickly located the Shoshone woman in her village. "I want to talk to you, my friend," said York in her tongue. She understood him, and they spoke in English and Shoshone. York asked her if she would guide his group through the West. She sat there a moment thinking; then she rose to her feet and said, "I will be your guide."

York was pleased with what he'd done. They needed a guide, and he had found an Indian woman to help them. "What is your name?" he asked.

"Sacagawea," she said, with a voice as peaceful as pine trees swayin' in a summer breeze.

York said the name to himself so he wouldn't forget. But it would have been nearly impossible to forget a name that belonged to such a woman as Sacagawea.

When York showed up back in town with their guide, the other men couldn't believe it.

"Where did you find her?" asked Meriwether Lewis, his bottom lip nearly dragging the ground.

"She is a Shoshone Indian, and she knows the place we're going very well," said York.

"Very good, York. You did a fine job," said Lewis, after pulling himself together.

Sacagawea looked dead level at the men and spoke: "The land up the Big River has been known to my people for many moons. I was a little girl when my grandmother took me there, and I have been back many times since. I will take you there."

"Well that settles that," William Clark said. "We have our guide."

In the spring of 1804, the Lewis and Clark expedition headed out of St. Louis up the Missouri River on a journey that both William Clark and York would remember for the rest of their lives. Lewis and Clark, York and Sacagawea paddled in boats way up the Missouri River, passing through parts of Kansas and Nebraska. All along the route, York proved his mettle. He had picked up many Indian tongues and was the party's best hunter, fisherman, and scout. You could see a change come over York each day as his confidence kept building. Sometimes the Indians they met thought this big black man was the leader, since York did most of the talking.

Winter started to close in on the party and Sacagawea led them to a friendly Indian village in North Dakota. "We must make camp nearby. It will be cold soon. If we go just up ahead, the Mandan Indians will let us stay with them," she said. When they reached the shore of the Mandan camp, young braves and chiefs stood on the banks to greet them.

"Do you think these Indians are really friendly?" asked a nervous Meriwether Lewis to William Clark.

"We'll soon find out. Look at the way they're looking at York. They are amazed," said a surprised Clark.

The Mandan Indians had never laid eyes on a black man, and York stood over six feet tall. At that time the average man was much smaller, so the Indians thought York was a great spirit. At these times, York played a major role in communicating with the Indians. He proved his skill with Indian sign language and used his blackness as a tool to get information that might not have been given to a white man.

"You are welcome here," said one of the chiefs after seeing York. "Come, follow me." Everyone stepped lively, following the Mandan to their camp.

That night was special for the Mandan Indians. After everybody ate, Clark decided to put on a show for them with the help of York.

"These people think you're from another world the way they look at you. Let's have a little fun. Remember how as children, we used to scare each other to death making animal noises? Let's delight our Indian friends. I'm sure they'll enjoy it," smiled William.

York didn't mind putting on a show for the Mandans. Fact was, he enjoyed all the attention. "I'll scare 'em to death," he laughed.

Clark called Sacagawea over and told her to get the attention of the chiefs and other Indians. "We have a special show for you, our Mandan friends. From far away we bring you a great spirit. He is from another land and has many powers," she said. York was standing next to her, and the Mandans sat in a circle around them both, waiting anxiously. York knew he would have some fun. As soon as Sacagawea finished her talk, York began his performance. Twisting his face, he roared like a mountain lion so loudly that one of the chiefs scrambled back fast, knocking over two or three Indians. York leaped so high in the air, that the Mandans caught their breaths, thinking he might not come down. Then he did a dance he used to do on the plantation and had all the Mandans clapping their hands. When he finished his show, they all ran over to him and rubbed his skin to see if it would come off.

"You are a great medicine man," shouted the chief. They were honored to have York and his party staying with them. To show their thanks, it was the custom of the Western Indians to offer wives, food, and a place to stay. To refuse was an insult. So the Lewis and Clark party stayed with the Mandans that winter before heading out in the spring to cross the Rocky Mountains.

By late March, the group was on the move again. The mountains of North Dakota rose up in the distance like crumpled velvet in the pink morning sky. Far away, eagles soared high in the air. The forests they passed through were untouched by any axe. The huge trees shot skyward and sheltered foxes, mountain lions, and birds that none of them had ever seen before. Young deer were so plentiful they stumbled over each other. The winds blew air so fresh throughout the plains it left a sweet taste in your mouth when you breathed it in.

William Clark was glad he made the trip. It had been hard, but the training they got back in St. Louis paid off. He and Lewis had mapped out much of the territory. They'd have some good information for the president when they got back. As he was reflecting on this, he couldn't help but think about his childhood friend York. In Virginia he was a slave, answering to Clark, but out here in the wild, he was a great man to the Indians. There was no way of getting around it: the party's life depended on a slave and an Indian woman.

That night as the party turned in, and York cleaned his knife and made ready for the next day, Sacagawea started talking to him. "We will reach the Big Mountains by

tomorrow noon. Many of my people live in those mountains,'' she said.

''They will be glad to see you,'' said a busy York.

''We may have a big problem. The Blackfeet, our enemy,
live around the foot of the Big Mountains. My people fear
them.''

The Big Mountains that Sacagawea kept talking about
were the Rocky Mountains. If the party was going to cross
over them, they needed information on how to do it so they
wouldn't lose any people.

''William, we need to get across these mountains before
the snow blocks the passes,'' said a nervous Meriwether
Lewis the next morning.

William Clark turned to Sacagawea. ''We need to know
how to get over those mountains. Can't you get your people
to help us?''

She had tried her best, but fear of the Blackfeet kept the
Shoshones in the hills. York had an idea: ''Tell them that a
powerful black man with great medicine has come up the
river in a canoe.'' York bet that his reputation had spread
throughout the territory from his stay with the Mandan
Indians.

''It's worth a try,'' smiled William Clark to his old
buddy. Quickly Sacagawea went back to her people and told
them the news.

''Look, I don't believe it,'' Lewis said after a few hours
time. ''They're actually coming down.''

I guess you could say the Shoshones's curiosity got the
best of them. They laid their fear aside to see this powerful
black man.

When the Shoshones saw York, they were indeed surprised. A couple of them carefully came over to rub his skin,

checking to see if he had covered himself with charcoal. York was getting used to this by now. It seemed like every Indian he met wanted to rub his skin. Once a Flathead Indian tried to explain to Lewis and Clark how his people saw York. "When we go into battle, the brave and victorious warrior paints his body in charcoal." That was how much they respected York. The Shoshones gave Clark and Lewis valuable information about how to cross the Rockies, all thanks to a slave named York, who was fast becoming a legend.

Once they crossed the Rocky Mountains, the party boated down the Columbia River. That wasn't an easy ride. The Columbia can be rough, and they had more than one close call. Several times they nearly lost a few men and their supplies. In November 1805 they reached the Pacific Ocean.

Around them they saw animals and plants never before seen by many white men. York stood at the mouth of the Columbia River and watched it flow into the Pacific. He had come a long way—from a slave in Virginia to somebody who was respected. Not only did he have equal say in where the party camped, but he was the main translator and bargained with the Indians so that the team could travel through their lands, sleep in their camps, and break bread with them. He knew that the party wouldn't have made it this far without his skills as hunter and interpreter.

After spending a hard winter at the mouth of the Columbia River, the Lewis and Clark crew packed up and started back to St. Louis. If you think about it, luck must have been on their side. All during their journey to the Pacific Ocean and back, they survived encounters with hostile Indians, snakes, storms, grizzly bears, and tricky mountain passes. Lewis and Clark wrote about all those glorious sights: They described all the territory from Missouri to the Pacific

Ocean, putting an end to the old belief that an easy route lay between Missouri and the Columbia River. Lewis kept track of the animals they saw and noted the different Indians they encountered. Best of all, of the forty-three men and one woman who began the trip in St. Louis, all except one (a fellow who died of sickness) returned to that same city on September 23, 1806.

Back in St. Louis, the men said their good-byes to one another, knowing they were part of something special. It was a journey none of them would ever forget.

William Clark said a special good-bye to Sacagawea. "I want to thank you. If there is anything I can ever do for you, send word and consider it done," he said.

"I'm honored to have been a part of this journey with you and your people. My spirit tells me much good will come from this, but it is York who deserves your praise. He is a powerful spirit," she said. Then they parted.

"So this is it. We've come to the end of our road. What are your plans?" Lewis asked Clark.

"Go back to Kentucky, I reckon," Clark said. "I'm not sure what I want to do, except for one thing—sleep in a *bed* for a change."

"Our report on this expedition should stand us in good stead with the president," Lewis said. "And what about York?" he continued. "What are you going to do about him?"

"I'm taking him with me. That is, if he wants to go," William Clark said.

York must have been thinking about his own future, too. Returning to slavery was impossible now.

"What you thinking 'bout, staring off into those hills?" said William Clark to York.

York was strangely quiet.

"You're a smart man. I knew that when we were little boys running around on my daddy's plantation. Sometimes I thought you were smarter than me. We couldn't have made this journey without you. I want you to know that. So when we get back to Kentucky, you got your freedom," Clark said. York leaned against a corral at the livery stable where he was keeping the horses. He turned, looked his childhood friend in the eyes and said, "Thank you. That's what I was thinking about."

York and William Clark stayed friends long after William freed him. Fact was, he got York started in a freight hauling business between Nashville and Richmond, Virginia. Some say York got tired of the business and began to get an itching for life in the wild and took off around 1832 to live with the Crows. I guess when you're respected and treated like somebody it's hard to go back to being treated like nobody. Now another story says that when York's hauling business died, he died around the same year, 1832. I tend to believe a well-known trapper named Zenas Leonard, who traveled through the Rocky Mountains after 1832. According to Zenas, he ran across a black man who told him he first came to that country with Lewis and Clark and returned to Missouri. Zenas said that this black man returned again with a trader named Mackinney and stayed in that country for twelve years, during which time he became chief of the Crows.

York followed his childhood friend into country where people never saw a black man before. They treated him with honor and respect. Many times the Lewis and Clark expedition would have been stopped dead in its tracks had it not been for a tall, strong black man named York.

"Sundown, just goes to show you, treat a man the way you want to be treated, nothing but kindness will follow you the rest of your life. York proved that when he went back into the wilderness and lived out his life with the Indians. Well, boy, it's been a long night. Old Man sun is starting to get up already. We better get some shut-eye, 'cause I got to fix that front door first thing in the morning."

ED "CUT NOSE" ROSE: FUR TRAPPER

The next morning the Old Cowboy and Sundown took the little baby goat out to the edge of a great meadow and let it go. On the far side of the meadow they saw a small herd of goats. One of them, probably the little goat's mother, baaed, and the little goat scampered off to join her.

Later on, the Old Cowboy hiked up into the hills to hunt for elk. Both he and Sundown were hungry. They hadn't brought a lot of food into the mountains with them because they had figured on bagging an elk. Sure enough, after a few hours, a fine young elk appeared, and the Old Cowboy took it down with his long iron. The Old Cowboy tied the elk to his horse and dragged it back to his cabin, where he carved and dressed the elk carcass into strips of fine steak.

By evening, he had cooked up a hearty meal of elk venison for both himself and Sundown. When they had finished eating, he settled back to smoke his pipe and tell a story. The sky had turned into a shimmering blanket of stars, and it seemed like they were the only souls in those mountains for miles around.

"Look at that sky," the Old Cowboy said, "and old Mr. Moon, shining so bright you'd almost think it's day." Sundown yawned and snuggled up against his old friend. When the Old Cowboy started talking like this, Sundown knew it was time for another story.

In the 1800s the Ohio Valley was overflowing with beaver, bear, mink, otter, and fox. The skins of these animals were worth a mint because they were prized by city folk back East and in Europe. As a result, white men from all over journeyed up the Mississippi River to seek their fortune trapping these animals. This was dangerous business for a white man because most of the animals were found deep in the hunting grounds of the Indians. A white man often needed help getting in and out of that land in one piece. To help them, African-American guides and trappers escorted the white hunters. These black hunters lived with the Indians and knew the ways of their people. Because they knew the land and were on friendly terms with the Indians, the black scouts acted as go-betweens for the white fur trading companies. One of these African Americans who knew the tribes and had a great reputation as a hunter was a big burly fellow named Edward Rose.

From what I gather, Ed Rose was born in Louisville, Kentucky. It's a little unclear when he was born, but by 1800 Ed was full grown and preparing to leave his home-town.

"Why you leavin' son?" his mama asked.

"Mama, I'm a grown man," Ed said as he put his belongings in a knapsack. "I got to find my way, and it ain't here in Kentucky."

"Do you know where you goin'?"

"I been talkin' to some of the boys in town. I'm gon' hitch on with them. They talkin' 'bout New Orleans."

"Why you want' go to N' Orleans?" Ed's mama asked.

Ed stopped packing for a minute. "Mama, the fellas tell me New Orleans got some of the prettiest women in the world, and there's money to be made in that town."

"What you gon' do? You ain't got no trade," she said.

"I'm big and strong mama. I'll find work; don't you worry none 'bout me."

"I figured one day you'd grow up and want to leave this place. When you was a little baby, you couldn't sit still for one hot minute," she said. Ed continued packing. "I suppose you know what you want. You keep yourself safe, and don't let no man run over you."

"I told the boys I'd meet them down by the river. We leaving today." He hugged his mother and left Kentucky, and to my recollection, he never came back.

Ed was big and strong for his age when he hitched up with those boys on a keelboat headed for New Orleans. They say he had Cherokee Indian and African blood running through his veins. Whatever he had in his blood, he turned out to be some kind of fighting man.

"Pull this boat over, we gonna stop here for a while," said one of the men traveling with Ed.

Ed pulled the boat over and tied it up alongside the dock of a little Mississippi River town. The three men had taken turns rowing all day. By now they needed some excitement.

Once on land, one of them pointed in the direction of a

saloon. "See that saloon? That's where I'm going. You boys with me? I could drink the whole Mississippi River," he said, laughing.

"Come on, Ed. You look like you need a little fun," said the other.

Ed smiled. "Ain't nothing to me. Let's go!"

When all three men walked in the saloon, everybody turned around. You'd thought it was a holdup or something because the place got as quiet as a graveyard. Ed and the other two men walked over to the bar.

"Me and my boys is mighty hungry. What you got to eat?" one fellow asked.

"Why don't you boys have a seat over there. I'll be over shortly," said the bartender.

They grabbed a table in the corner. Ed kept his back to the wall. That way he could see everything in front of him. In those days, if a stranger walked into an unknown bar, he'd better be equally as good with his fists as he was with a gun, otherwise he'd get beat up and robbed. Ed and his friends were strangers in a saloon full of white men. It wasn't unusual to see a black man in the company of white trappers in those days, because they were often used as guides. But three black men in an all-white saloon—that could be very dangerous.

"Something ain't right. I can feel it," said Ed.

"Me too," whispered the other one.

All of them had good instincts. In those days your life depended on you sizing up a situation. Right about then, all three men felt a little uneasy with the stares they were getting.

"What will you boys have?" asked the bartender.

"Steak for everybody. We powerful hungry," the shorter fellow said. By now Ed had noticed that two men, whose hands rested on the handles of their hunting knives, had slid over to the saloon door. A big giant-sized fellow had moved to the end of the bar close to their table. Shaking like a leaf in a Texas tornado, the bartender could barely speak. "We're out of steaks, sorry."

"What you mean you out of steaks? That man over there is chewin' on one!" Ed said.

"We ain't got no more! Can't you hear!" spoke the giant-sized fellow.

Looking as solid as a hundred-year-old oak, Ed got to his feet. His blood was boiling hotter than a Mexican red pepper, and he wanted to put that big fellow down. By that time the other two fellows with Ed had kicked back their chairs. The shorter one had his pistol ready as he checked the crowd.

"You boys a bit outnumbered, ain't ya? Why don't you just empty yo' pockets," cackled the big stranger.

Ed never blinked an eye when he said, "Why don't you just try an' make us, mister."

The giant stranger looked Ed over. He wasn't used to nobody giving him any lip. His size alone made most men shake in their boots, but Ed wasn't moving one bit. "You kinda young to die so soon," the big man said as he took off his coat. "I'm going to give you a whippin' you ain't never gonna forget."

Ed just looked at him and smiled as he moved to the center of the saloon, "Do it!" he challenged.

The giant stranger took a swing at Ed, and a noise that sounded like timber falling in an open meadow rocked the saloon. Too bad he missed with that looping right hook. Ed saw it coming, ducked, and came back up with a right cross. The room shook as Ed's fist clipped the giant stranger smack dab on the chin, knocking him over a table and through a side window. Nobody moved. You'd thought a witch had put a spell on everybody; they had never seen such power come from one man.

"It's time boys to get on down the road," said the short fellow. As they backed out of that saloon, the men guarding the doorway cleared a path like a herd of runaway buffalo.

"Didn't know you could hit like that, boy," said one of the fellows as they continued on down the Mississippi.

"I ain't never had to show nobody," replied Ed.

"You sho' know how to handle yourself for a young boy. You ain't going to have no trouble in New Orleans," laughed the short fellow.

Once they got to New Orleans, Ed waved good-bye to his river companions. "You boys take it easy. This is where I get off."

"What you plan on doin', Ed?," asked one of the fellows.

"Ain't figured it out yet. I suppose I got plenty of time to think about it." That was the last Ed Rose saw of those men; he had come to New Orleans to find all the adventure life had to offer.

New Orleans welcomed Ed Rose like a lost sheep returning to the fold. As he stood there on the levee, his eyes gazed from east to west and took in more people in one place than he'd ever seen in his whole life. The marketplace was rich with the smells of wild ducks strung up on sticks, oysters, fresh fish, bananas, piles of oranges, apples, and ears of corn. The varieties of food was only matched by the different types of people trying to sell their wares. Ed saw black men and women of every hue, from deep dark brown to pecan tan, plus Indians, whites, and all shades in between. As he continued to walk, he heard so many different languages it made him giddy. It seemed like everyone wanted him to buy something. There must have been over five hundred sellers and buyers crowded together, all trying to out-shout each other. Ed took it all in stride while carrying his knapsack on his shoulder with one hand and using his free arm like the rudder on a ship, steering his way through an ocean of people. He'd find out what this town had to offer. So far he liked what he saw.

The river boat gambling and night life that Ed found in New Orleans fit him like a glove. See, New Orleans was one of the few Southern towns that had large numbers of freed blacks, and the scent of freedom soon infected Ed. The idea of working somebody else's land didn't have the same appeal for him as those pretty river boats floating up and down the Mississippi.

A river boat was a stately vision on the water. Some had three or more levels, and to Ed, each boat seemed more beautiful than the other. There were always pretty women on board and lively banjo music could be heard on shore as the boat passed by. I guess it's no mystery why Ed found life on the river a lot more fun than working on somebody's farm.

Ed had a bit of a temper and it wasn't long before he developed a reputation as a fighter. Everybody up and down the Mississippi River knew of this big strapping young black man named Ed Rose. When you build a reputation as a fighter like Ed did, you draw all kinds of unsavory characters who want to test you.

One night on the river boat, rumors of a fight got as thick as the smoke from those Havana cigars you'd always see jammed in the mouths of the fancy gamblers. It seemed that another man, Mike Fink, who was also known for his fighting habits, was on board.

Ed had heard of Mike but the two men had never crossed paths. People would brag that Ed could whip Mike, and some folks argued that Mike could tan Ed's hide.

It was hotter than it had ever been that summer night on the Mississippi and crowds were everywhere you turned. The gambling was heavy and so was the drinking. One gambler, dressed in white linen and diamond studs, was winning every hand at the poker table from some poor soul who was down on his luck.

"You ought to call it quits, mister, while you still got the shirt on your back," said the gambler.

"You take a marker?" said the fellow who was losing.

"Sorry, just cash," replied the gambler.

By this time the fellow losing made one last try to get his money back. Scratching his chin like a hound dog with fleas, he said, "If you're really a gambler, I'll wager a thousand dollars that Ed Rose can whip Mike Fink."

Everybody stopped what they were doing and all eyes were glued to the two gamblers at their table.

"You ain't got a thousand dollars, mister," said the gambler.

The other fella pulled off his fancy ring and gold pocket watch. "That ought to cover it," he said.

"I'll take a piece of that," said a man in the crowd.

"Me too," said somebody else, and before you knew it everybody was betting on Mike Fink or Ed Rose.

"Hold your horses!" shouted the gambler. "How are we gonna get these two men to fight?"

"I've got an idea," said the fellow who made the bet. "I'll be right back." He jumped up from his chair and disappeared down the stairs. After asking around, he found Mike Fink in the company of a few ladies. Fink, as usual, was bragging about his exploits.

"Excuse me, Mister Fink. May I speak to you a moment?" the fellow asked.

"I'm busy" said Mike, as he turned to the ladies.

"I see that, but I thought you ought to know . . . there's a rumor goin' round that you're hiding from Ed Rose, and that you're also afraid of him. People are betting you won't show your face anywhere near him."

By that time, Mike had grabbed that fellow by his shirt with both hands and lifted him off the ground and was about to throw him into the Mississippi. "You get Ed Rose to meet me, and we'll see who's afraid to show whose face. Now get out of my sight" said a pretty riled up Mike Fink, as he slammed the fellow down on the deck so hard he nearly went through it.

Ed Rose was pleased when word reached him that Mike Fink was looking for him. He knew their paths would cross one day, and now was as good a time as any to settle the rumor about who had the best hands. "Mike says you hiding from him," said one of Ed's boys. "I ain't going nowhere," Ed responded. "Mike wants me; he can find me."

Except for a tiny circle in the middle where both Mike and Ed stood, the open deck at the end of the boat was packed tighter than the skin on an Indian tom-tom drum. Ed had one of his boys next to him, and some of Mike's people were standing at his side. It was the first time either man had seen each other, but they sure knew about the other's reputation. Mike was a big, ol' white country boy who knew how to use his hands, and there he stood facing a big strapping black man known to swing one powerful punch.

It didn't take much to get them started. They didn't like each other much. My guess is all that talk about who had the best hands must of got on their nerves. A dust-up was one way to end all the talk. They didn't waste much time getting at it. Ed and Mike rolled around the floor like two giant boulders rolling downhill. People who stood too close got knocked down like match sticks in a wind storm. Both men landed blows so heavy they sounded like claps of thunder on an open prairie. They punched each other up one side of the deck and down the other before something happened. As tough as Mike Fink was, the blows he took from Ed Rose started to weaken him. Figuring he was losing, Mike wrestled Ed to the ground and bit off the tip of his nose. Ed let out a yell that nearly woke up the dead. He picked Mike up and threw him over the rail and into the river. From that day on, Ed was known as "Cut Nose" Rose. I never did hear anymore about Mike Fink after that. He may have lost the fight, but he left a mark on Ed Rose that stayed with him the rest of his life.

Not too long after that showdown on the riverboat, Ed began to hanker for a new way of living. He had been up and down that old river for a long time, and the gambling life didn't hold his attention like it once had. Around the spring of 1806, Ed hopped off the riverboat for good in St. Louis again. There he hooked up with the best group of trappers operating along the Osage River in Kansas and Missouri.

Ed took to the hunter's life like a duck takes to water. His trapper friends taught him everything they knew. They were surprised at how quickly young Ed picked up the trade. By the end of the year, Ed was a seasoned hunter and fur trapper and knew the Osage like the back of his hand.

After a year in the wilderness, Ed returned to St. Louis again. He was low on money and looking for a way to pick up some quick cash. On his way from the livery stable to the local saloon, he passed a group of men.

"I hear this Manuel Lisa fella is looking for a guide to go

up the Yellowstone River into Crow country," said one man.

"Sure 'nuff," replied the other. "And the pay is pretty good, too."

Now Ed had spent most of his money gambling and on other foolishness, and he wasn't even sure he could pay for his meal after putting new shoes on his horse. Always eager for a new adventure and smart enough to see an opening for a quick dollar, he stopped and asked one of the men a question. "Excuse me for buttin' in, but did you say a man is looking for a guide?"

One fellow looked at Ed like he was trying to place where he knew him from. "You a guide, young fella?" he asked.

Standing tall and straight as an arrow, Ed replied, "I know these parts like an eagle knows how to fly. Now where is this man that's doing the hiring?"

"He's having supper right now in that cafe," continued the man, as he pointed out the place.

"Thank ya, fellas. What's his name?" smiled Ed.

"Mr. Manuel Lisa, and he don't like to be bothered when he's eating supper," continued the man. But Ed didn't pay any attention to that last part; he was already four strides on his way to the cafe.

Manuel Lisa was having his supper with some friends and he didn't notice Ed Rose until a waitress came to his table.

"Excuse me, Mr. Manuel Lisa," she said, "there's a man at the bar that says he has an important message for you."

Manuel Lisa looked up from his steak and beans and squinted through the smoky light to see the man the waitress had mentioned. There were a lot of men at the bar, but at last he saw the man he was looking for. He was a big fellow who looked like he had been carved out of a mountain, and he stared back at Manuel with a funny look on his face.

Manuel gave Ed a devil-may-care grin. "Tell the man I'm busy," he said to the waitress. By the time he finished the sentence, Ed had started walking over to Manuel's table. One of Manuel's men wanted to jump up, but remained in his chair when Ed said, "Sit down or that be the last time you ever move!"

"Who are you?" asked Manuel.

"I'm Ed Rose, your new guide."

"My guide!" replied a surprised Manuel Lisa. "Who told you I needed a guide?"

"You wanna go up the Yellowstone River where no white man has been before, you better know how to talk to the Crows," said Ed.

Manuel Lisa was impressed. This bronze hunk of timber had read his mind. The Crows did have a fearsome reputation, and if a man wanted to trap for grizzly and fox in that rich country, he had to reckon with that band of Indians. "So what do you know about that place?" Lisa asked.

"I know them parts like a hound dog on the scent of sly fox," bragged Ed, "and I speak Crow."

Now Ed was part right and part wrong. He knew the territory, but he didn't speak Crow. See, Ed had more courage than ten grizzly bears, and he was as smart as prairie wolf and just as mean. After he told you something, there was no doubt in his mind he could do it.

"Tell you what I'll do," Manuel Lisa said. "If you know Crow like you say, I'll give you a percentage of our catch. But if you're lying, I'll see to it you don't speak Crow or any other language. Get your things together; we move out in the morning."

Mr. Lisa was lucky to still be alive after talking to Ed like that. If Ed hadn't needed the job, no telling what he would have done to him. No man ever tried to put fear in Ed Rose, and no man could.

The next morning, Ed, Manuel, and the rest of the party sailed up the Missouri River in a keelboat on a journey that led them through Kansas, Nebraska, South Dakota, North Dakota, and into Montana. This land was plentiful. The rivers overflowed with fresh fish of every kind, and deer and other wild game stumbled over each other because their numbers were so large. With each passing day Manuel Lisa got happier and happier, thinking about all the money he'd make from the rich furs he'd take back to his Missouri Fur company. Five or six weeks later, they reached the mouth of the Big Horn River, which fed into the Yellowstone. The group stopped there and started cutting down timber to build a place they called Fort Manuel. It would be the first trading post in the heart of Crow country on the upper Yellowstone River.

A month or two passed before the men finished building Fort Manuel and several other camps within a few miles of the fort. By now a few of the men had ventured out on their own, and felt they knew the country as well as Ed did. At one of the camps, Ed warned three fellows about straying out too far away from the main post.

"You fellas better stay close to camp the next couple of days. The moon will be full, and the Crows will be out looking for game," warned Ed.

"We been out here for months and I ain't seen hide nor hair of no Crow Indians. I'm tired of taking orders from you anyway. Since when did a black man talk uppity to whites. Me and my partner will do as we please without any say from you," one of the men said.

"When the Crows go on the war-path you'll turn your

hides back in this direction as fast as your short legs can carry you. I'm telling you, when the moon is full, things happen out here you white people ain't never seen.''

''You're just trying to put fear in us,'' said the big, strapping white fellow. ''Ain't nothing happened, and ain't nothing gonna happen. We're gonna get all the furs we can, no matter how we get them.''

That next morning the men were shaken out of their sleep by yells that sounded like coyotes barking. ''What's that?'' shouted one of the men. Before Ed could tell him to get down, an arrow hit his chest, and he fell to the ground like a sack of potatoes.

''Take cover!'' Ed shouted. This time nobody gave him any back-talk. They scrambled for cover like rats scrambling from a sinking ship. Nobody saw where the arrow came from, but clearly the Crows were mad about something. The Crows hadn't attacked with all their warriors, which meant only one thing: something had been taken from them, and they wanted it back. If it wasn't returned soon they would kill everybody.

''What's going on!'' shouted Manuel Lisa, who was visiting that camp to check on the quality of the furs.

''Somebody got something that don't belong to 'em,'' said Ed.

''What do you mean? We have a right to trap here!'' screamed Manuel Lisa.

''Trapping is one thing. They don't mind that. But somebody took from them; that made them mad,''said Ed. Ed noticed that the two men who had strayed away from the camp were as quiet as prairie rats. They looked at one another but didn't say nothing. What Ed didn't know, but suspected, was that the day before, the men had come across some Crow traps and stole the furs. See, Crows only trapped for food and for clothing to help them get through those cold winters. Manuel Lisa's men were out there for money, and they didn't care who they made it from.

"You two!" shouted Ed from behind a boulder, "Y'all took some furs from Crow traps, didn't you?"

"What makes you think we took anything. Maybe they're here to steal our furs," one of them shouted back.

"Where are the furs?" Ed shouted again.

The other man pointed to where they had stashed them, and Ed, dodging bullets and arrows, crawled on his belly to where the furs were hidden. He quickly found a handful of unmarked furs. These belonged to the Crows, who had a different way of trapping animals, one that left no markings on the inside of the hide.

Standing up tall, in plain view, Ed held the furs over his head for all to see. From out of nowhere Crow Indians came from behind trees and rocks. It looked like the sky had rained Crows; there must have been a hundred or more. Majestically, Ed walked toward the Indians carrying those furs over his head, while Manuel Lisa and his men watched, knowing their lives depended on what came out of Ed Rose's mouth. Reaching deep inside his memory, Ed searched his brain for the right word to calm the Crow chief. Now remember, he didn't know how to speak the Crow language, but he did speak Cherokee. That was the language he was going to use to talk to the chief, and he hoped the chief would understand at least his peaceful intent even if he might not follow every one of Ed's words. He stopped about ten feet from an Indian who looked like the leader. Ed spoke with all the confidence of a man in charge, "I am part Cherokee; I guided these white men to your hunting grounds. One hunter took these animals from your traps. Now I must give you back your furs—and more."

Turning in Manuel's direction, he yelled, ''Give them more furs or we all may die.'' Grudgingly, Manuel signaled to two men, who gathered up a couple of arm loads of furs and slowly dropped them at Ed's feet. Better to live to trap another day, Manuel figured, than die in a camp full of furs.

The Crows started mumbling amongst themselves, and Ed could make out just enough to sense that gift of extra furs wasn't going to satisfy these Crows. Right about then, one of the biggest Crow Indians Ed ever saw stepped out from the crowd and put himself in Ed's face. Holding a tomahawk, he took off his hunting gear and stripped down to a deer skin covering. Ed had to fight and win, or he and the rest of Manuel's party would die. Stepping back about a yard and a half, Ed pulled off his shirt. When the Indian saw those muscles, his eyes nearly popped out of his head.

Ed didn't have nothing to fight with but his bare hands. The men circled each other warily when, like lightning, the Indian swung at Ed's head and missed. The power of that swing made the Crow lose his balance, and faster than a hungry rattlesnake striking its prey, Ed caught the Indian with a thundering right cross that sent the Indian in one direction and his tomahawk in another. You'd thought a tree fell when that Indian hit the ground, and like a fallen tree, he didn't move one bit. Some of the Crows moved in a close circle around Ed. The leader put forth his hand. Ed knew what that meant; he grabbed the chief's hand and they both shook. Manuel Lisa breathed easier now. He figured the Indians would leave now that Ed had knocked out their biggest brave.

''You are a great fighter. You fight like a Crow. Come with us,'' said the chief.

Ed turned to Manuel Lisa. ''I'll be back after the winter, with more furs than your eyes have ever seen.''

"You're going with them?" Lisa asked.

"Don't worry 'bout me. I know the ways of these folks. Besides, I can't rightly insult them again. We might not get a second chance."

The big brave finally got up and was told something in Crow. He gave Ed his horse, and Ed and the rest of the Indians rode off with the furs. The brave who lost the fight ran behind them all the way back to their camp.

Ed took to living with the Crows like a baby calf to his mother's milk. Anything a Crow could do, Ed mastered. He finally became so good that he outhunted them and rode bareback better than the most seasoned Crow. And when it came to hand-to-hand fighting, no Crow Indian stood a chance against him. He also learned to speak Crow and learned Indian sign language. The Crows came to depend on Ed's bargaining skills at the white trading posts. Through him, they got better trades for their furs. And Ed also had led them to victory in a war with their most hated enemy, the Blackfeet. Finally, the Crows decided to reward him for his exploits.

"You showed us how to fight, to hunt like a fox, and you war dance like a deer. You are sly at the trading post. We make better trades because of you. Our council has decided to make you chief," said the Crow leader. See, the Crow Indians, like some of the other Indian people, didn't judge you by the color of your skin. If you could beat them in anything, you were a chief. Ed proudly took on the role of chief of the Crow Indians and spent the winter learning everything he could about them.

Ed stayed on as chief of the Crows for roughly three years before taking off again. Ed knew his skills as a guide were in demand by many white hunters looking for virgin trapping grounds, so he began plying his trade as a guide, hunter, and interpreter for the Rocky Mountain Fur Company of William Ashley and the American Fur Company of John Jacob Astor.

He trapped and hunted with those outfits for a few years, and when he got bored, just like a big piece of tumble weed, he'd roll on to the next place . . . wherever the wind blew him. He bounced around the Missouri River territory for a few more years, then came back to New Orleans. Then he'd tire of New Orleans and head right back to the Crow Indians. With the Crows his word was law; to them he was the greatest of all chiefs.

His luck started to turn sour around 1823, when he fell into the hands of the Blackfeet. Nobody knows what actually happened, but my guess is Ed was out hunting all by himself when they surprised him. It was a rule of the Blackfeet Indians to give any brave, captured enemy warrior a hundred-step head start to save his life. When Ed had taken his hundredth step, the Blackfeet took off after him. Now the Blackfeet were strong and brave warriors and knew about Ed Rose, so they had to make sure he didn't get away. Ed dashed for the woods as fast as he could, but the Blackfeet headed him off. Like a young pony, he cut to the left and made a strong run for the river and dove in. Swimming like a fish underwater, Ed came up in a small air pocket underneath a log jam. The Blackfeet scrambled all over those logs looking for him, but they couldn't find Ed.

"We burn you out Cut Nose," shouted one of the Indians. They set fire to the logs and waited with their rifles to shoot whatever came up for air. But after a while, the Blackfeet got tired of waiting. "We give you one more chance if you come out now," shouted one of the Blackfeet.

Ed knew the game they were playing and kept his mouth shut. After some time had passed, the Blackfeet figured that not even the great Cut Nose could withstand all that smoke and fire, so they rode off thinking he was finally dead.

"During the next eight years or so, Ed must of got into more close calls than there are stars in the sky. Sundown, there's just no telling what eventually happened to him. Stories go around that he died in battle fighting with the Crow Indians against the Blackfeet. But I don't think anybody rightly knows for sure. Just when you thought you figured out how he died, like the prairie wolf he'd show up again and slip right through your fingers.

"He left a hard row to hoe for those men that came after him. Ed was one of the first men ever to go deep into the Rocky Mountains, testing his will and cunning against the unkown and the forces of nature. When tales are spun around campfires, you only hear about white fellows like Jim Bridger, Jed Smith, William Ashley, and Kit Carson. Fact is, Ed Rose was a seasoned trapper when these gents were still little boys. Sundown, you alright, boy? Look at that sky, looks like rain to me. We better be heading on inside. Tomorrow I want to take you to the mountaintop. Up there it seems like you can see forever, and I've got something I want to show you."

ALVIN COFFEY AND THE CALIFORNIA GOLD RUSH

The next day at the crack of dawn the Old Cowboy shook himself awake, packed a few strips of smoked elk meat in his pack, and started up the path to the mountaintop. He and Sundown hiked through thick pine and fir forests for most of the morning to get there. The forests abruptly ended about half an hour before they came to the top. At this point they entered a huge meadow of grasses and rock. They had crossed the tree line, the altitude above which trees could not grow. All around them they could see the peaks of mountains in the distance.

"Look over yonder, Sundown," the Old Cowboy said, pointing west. "If you look hard enough you can see all the way to California... or at least that's sure how it seems to me."

The Old Cowboy sat down against a large boulder, lit his pipe, and began to talk.

California has always stood for something real special. You see, as far back as the 1840s the West was as wide open as a barnyard door on a sunny day. There just weren't too many people living out here. California was a real quiet place. There were only two towns there of any size—Los Angeles in the south and San Francisco in the north. San Francisco was set on a hilly strip of land between the ocean and a beautiful bay. It was a quiet and peaceful town with a mild, pleasing climate. The main business of the town was the sea trade that passed through its small port.

Then in 1848, a white man named James Marshall discovered some gold nuggets while building a sawmill for his boss, John Sutter. Marshall and Sutter tried to keep their find quiet, and for almost a year they succeeded. But in 1849 their secret was discovered. After that, San Francisco and the hills further inland were stampeded by gold-hungry prospectors. These "Forty-Niners" poured into the state, swelling its population till it resembled an overstuffed pig after feeding time.

San Francisco just wasn't prepared for the large numbers of people who landed on her shores. Soon the town was littered for miles around with tent cities. Buildings went up faster than greased lightning. Herds of people traveled from the city to the mining sites, turning the main streets into seas of mud.

In this crush of people, fighting broke out—especially between white and black miners. For one thing, many white miners didn't want to dig for gold alongside a black man. To these people, mining looked too much like the kind of work slaves did, and this kind of white man didn't want to be seen looking like a slave. On the other hand, some white folks held the funny notion that black miners had magical powers that could lead them to gold. It wasn't surprising that people who believed this superstitious nonsense also wanted laws passed to keep blacks out of the mining country.

Finally, black gold miners who worked as slaves for their masters couldn't claim any of the gold they found. Only freed black men could claim their gold. Even if a black man made a "strike," he had to be very careful with his money, especially in town. The law still favored the white man, and more than one black gold miner lost his money to some white fellow who told the sheriff that the black man was his slave. But none of this stopped black prospectors from striking it rich. I remember one man named Alvin Coffey.

Alvin Coffey was born into slavery and ended up on a plantation in Missouri owned by a Dr. Bassett. In 1849, when he was just twenty-seven, Coffey got the news from his master that they soon would be going to California to try their luck in the gold fields. Coffey had been married now for several years. He and his wife had two lovely daughters, but Dr. Bassett would not be taking the whole family to California. He only needed Alvin.

"When will you be back?" asked Coffey's wife.

"I don't know. Master Bassett say we be out there 'till we strike it rich. I tell you one thing. I'm goin' to make enough money to buy our freedom," said Coffey.

"Where is California?" asked his curious wife.

Coffey kept packing his things as he was thinking. "It's out West somewhere. I overheard Master Bassett talking to one of the other plantation owners, and all I kept hearing him say was California is rich with gold. I guess Master Bassett figured he would get his share."

"So why is he taking you?" she asked.

"Now you know he ain't gonna mine for no gold—not if he got me to do the work. But that's alright. Like I said, once I make the money I'm gon' do like I hear some of the other slaves have done—buy our freedom."

"Master Bassett ain't gon' let you do that," she said.

"If I make him a big enough offer, I be dog-gone if he don't take it," replied Coffey. "You keep them two girls of mine in line while their daddy's away. When I come back we all gon' be free. Now I best be gettin' me some sleep. We head out of here at the crack of dawn. You just keep remembering what I say—we ain't gon' be slaves forever."

Alvin Coffey blew out the little flame in the lantern that dimly lit their small slave quarters and kissed his wife goodnight. The next morning before the rooster crowed, Master Bassett and Alvin Coffey saddled up for California to strike it rich.

Coffey and Dr. Bassett rode into San Francisco smack dab in the middle of the gold rush. Everywhere they turned people flooded the streets. There were black men, yellow men, white men, all wearing dirty clothes and carrying pick-axes. Long lines snaked out of the general stores; music from the saloons spilled into the streets along with a few miners who had too much to drink. Mules, loaded down with every type of mining tool ever made, headed out of town in lines four rows deep. For a young slave from Missouri, this was some sight.

"You watch the horses. I'm going over to that claims office and see what's left around here to work," said Dr. Bassett.

As he waited with the horses Alvin watched an "old-timer" carrying a shovel. This older man seemed to notice Coffey and stopped.

"How y'all doin' young fella?," he inquired.

"I'm doin' just fine. You sho' look happy," said Coffey.

"I ought to be. See that white man over there," he shouted, pointing across the way. "I just paid him fifteen hundred dollars for my freedom!"

"Well, ain't that somethin'," Alvin said, smiling.

The old-timer just shook his head. He was almost too thrilled to talk. By and by though, he told Alvin a bit about mining and how slaves were buying their freedom in California. When Dr. Bassett came out of the claims office he brushed by the old-timer and mounted up without saying a word to the black man.

"Let's get!" said Bassett. The newly freed black man looked at Alvin sympathetically.

"You take care, young fella," he shouted.

As Coffey and Dr. Bassett rode out of town, Alvin's mind worked overtime, thinking about what the old-timer had told him. Freedom was something he wanted now more than anything. The look on that old-timer's face was worth more than all the gold in California. Somehow, no matter how long it took, he knew he and his family would be free.

The two men made up camp about fifteen miles outside of town. That evening, after supper, Dr. Bassett called Coffey over.

"You been mighty quiet. What's on your mind?" asked Dr. Bassett.

"I been thinkin' 'bout gettin' an early start in the mornin'. We got to get to work before all that gold is gone," laughed Coffey.

"So you can't wait to get started mining for gold. What's your hurry? You ain't going nowhere," Dr. Bassett said, as the smoke from his pipe curled around his head like a coiling rattlesnake. "I heard that black fella back in town talking about being free. Is that what's on your mind?''

"Yes sir," Coffey said. "It's something a man thinks about."

"You help me get rich," Dr. Bassett said, "and I'll see what I can do for you."

Alvin Coffey just looked at his master, giving him a slight smile. He didn't know whether he could trust Dr. Bassett, but he didn't have any other choice at the moment.

"Where do we start?" he asked, pointing at a map Bassett held in his hands.

Trying to read Coffey's face, Dr. Bassett gave him a long look before he spoke. "You'll start digging over there in the foothills of those mountains. According to the claims office, that's open territory," he said.

Even though Coffey and his master had their claims, they weren't out there all alone. Other miners were digging right next to them. But these fellows left him alone, and he worked steadily, digging at his site.

Mining for gold was hard work, but Alvin Coffey had a strong back and a vision of freedom that he held in his heart. Not only did he work all day mining gold for his master, but at night to earn some extra money he washed clothes for the nearby miners. I reckon his master must have realized his slave's value. Coffey and Bassett had been out there a year, and so far Coffey had brought in over $3,500. Dr. Bassett knew why Coffey worked so hard. Stories about slaves buying their freedom continued to circulate throughout the California mining fields, and these stories made Dr. Bassett uneasy.

Every few weeks Coffey and Bassett ran out of supplies at their camp. Working as hard as Alvin did, mining tools and food staples were used up pretty fast. One day, Coffey noticed supplies were running low.

"I'm going into town and stock up on some dry goods. We gettin' slim on supplies," he told Dr. Bassett.

"You hurry back," Bassett said. "There's still some light left. We can dig some more before nightfall."

"Yes, sir. I'll be back before you can count all your fingers," laughed Coffey as he rode off to town.

By now the general store manager was pretty familiar with most of the miners. He'd seen Coffey in the store before with his master. Dr. Bassett let it be known that Coffey was his property.

"How you doing, Coffey? You fellas strike the big one yet?" asked the manager.

"We still digging away, trying every day. Next time I see you, I'm gon' buy everything in the place. Then you know for sure, I hit the big one," joked Coffey.

"I guess you heard about old Jake. He hit a vein of gold so big, he left here for Los Angeles. He said he was going to raise cattle," said the manager.

Coffey knew old Jake. He was a slave Coffey had met shortly after arriving from Missouri. Coffey wondered how much of the gold old Jake was able to keep. I guess he figured whatever the amount, Jake must have kept enough for himself after paying for his freedom.

"You got everything you need?" the manager asked. "We got some brand new pans for you to wash away the sand from all that gold packed in them hills."

"You still tryin' to get me to spend more of Master Bassett's money. I got all the pans I need right now, thank you!" laughed Coffey as he paid for his supplies with gold dust. As Coffey left the general store, he noticed two men arguing and pointing fingers at each other in the street. He wouldn't have paid them much attention, except one man was a young black miner and the other was a neatly dressed white fellow who Coffey hadn't seen before.

"I saw you steal that sack from my saddlebag. Now hand it over!" demanded the white man.

"Mister, I don't know you, but I've worked these hills a long time. You ask anybody in this town, and they tell you—Lester ain't no thief! This is my gold and I ain't givin' it to you or nobody!" said the black miner.

"You don't use that tone of voice to me. You're nothing but a slave, and you know better than to talk to me like that. Now hand over that sack," the white man said. As the white tenderfoot reached to take the sack from the black miner's hand, he was met with a thundering left hook that sent him flying backwards a good ten feet. He landed smack dab on his back and stayed there. A crowd of rough-looking white men saw the fight. Two of them leaped off their horses, grabbed pick axe handles from their saddlebags, and ran over to the black miner. The black miner quickly put his gold in his saddle bags, turned, and met the two white men head on. One swung for the miner's head and missed. The black miner took away this man's axe handle and blocked a blow coming from the other white fellow.

Not knowing what to do, Coffey watched the fight as he stood outside the general store. If he tried to help the black miner, he might have got himself killed. Still, the next time he could have been in that man's place. By now, a half-dozen more white men had jumped into the fracas to attack the miner. The black man fought with the bravery of a wounded lion, but the odds were more than he could handle. The miner took one, then another pick-axe blow to the head and body, but for each of these blows he delivered a blow back to his attackers. By now, three of the white attackers lay unconscious on the ground.

The manager of the store had come out to the sidewalk and stood next to Coffey. "Do you know who that white man is, Coffey?" he asked.

"No, sir. I sure don't. I've never seen him before."

"Me neither," the manager said. "But I do know Lester."

"And is he an honest man?" Coffey asked.

"As honest as old Jake was," said the manager.

"Then this ain't right what they're doin' to him," Coffey said.

"It's best to stay out of it, Coffey," the manager said.

But Coffey's anger had reached a boil. He had set down the goods he bought at the store and grabbed a shovel from a display stand near the door.

"Now just you wait here a moment," the manager said to Alvin.

Coffey took a step forward just as a shot rang out like a clap of thunder. The young miner fell to his knees. Across the street a cowboy stood with a smoking revolver in his hands. He aimed and fired once more, and the miner crumpled to the ground. He lay dead, face down in the dirt. Alvin dropped the shovel, and with tears in his eyes, loaded up the horses and left town.

He had a lot to think about on that ride back to camp. His mind reflected on the young black miner who had been shot down in the street trying to protect his gold, and he thought about old Jake starting a new life in Los Angeles. He'd heard stories about Los Angeles from some freed blacks that came up north to pan for gold. They told him how the laws against holding blacks as slaves were strongly enforced in Los Angeles and that a black man had a better chance to make a new start there. Coffey thought about something else, too—

his family. He wanted them to see this part of the country. California was dangerous, but so was Missouri and many other parts of the country for black people. Besides the danger, though, California was beautiful: there were secret hills tucked behind the shadows of giant mountains, rivers with fish so plentiful you could just reach in and grab what you wanted, and rich green meadows overflowing with wild game of every kind. Most of all, though, a fellow had to grab the chance of being free. Coffey decided when he got back to camp, he would ask Dr. Bassett how much longer they planned to stay. Then he'd make an offer to buy his freedom and that of his family. Two years had passed pretty quickly since both men had arrived in San Francisco and Coffey figured he must have brought in at least $5,000 worth of gold for Dr. Bassett. He also had managed to put away about $700 from washing clothes.

In the evening of the next day, after a hard day's work, Coffey screwed up his courage to talk to Dr. Bassett. Their claim was producing gold, but so far they hadn't hit a strike. Both men had finished their meal, and the light from the campfire cast shadowy images against their canvas tents as Coffey began to speak.

"Seems like we been out here a long time, sir. I 'spect we made 'bout as much as this here claim gonna put out. What you think?" said Coffey.

"Hmmm, what?" said Dr. Bassett as he looked up from some papers he was reading.

"I say, I 'spect we be moving on soon," replied Coffey.

"Yeah, I'm planning on going further north. We've worked this claim to the bone. Ain't nothing left," said Bassett.

"You know something, sir. The way I figured, I worked and made you over five thousand in gold, and with the extra

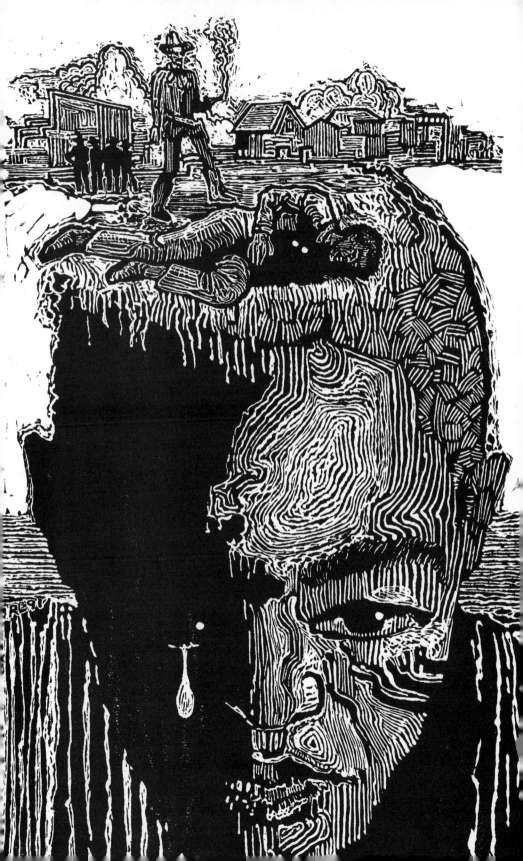

money I save from washing clothes, that ought to pay for me and my family's freedom,'' said Coffey.

Dr. Bassett sat there with ''thinking'' written all over his face. ''You know you are absolutely right. You made me about five thousand, but that's hardly enough money to buy your freedom and that of your wife and two daughters. In fact, you owe me money. I brought you out here, fed you . . .''

Coffey cut in. ''I paid you for my food from the extra money I made at night washin' clothes.''

''Just how much did you make?'' asked Dr. Bassett.

Coffey didn't want to tell him anything else, but Dr. Bassett held his wife and family as slaves back in Missouri, and this was one trump card he'd play if he had to.

''You just might have enough for a down payment for your wife, now how much?'' asked the sly Dr. Bassett.

''Seven hundred dollars, that's all I got,'' said Coffey.

''That's a start. When we get back to Missouri, we'll see about your freedom. Of course, I want the extra money first,'' he continued. Coffey didn't trust him, but he was caught between the devil and his pitch fork, so he gave Dr. Bassett the extra money he'd saved in those two years of washing clothes.

After that conversation, Dr. Bassett wasted little time in getting back to Missouri. It was a long and dangerous trip through mountain passes and across swollen rivers and Indian country, but by spring, just six weeks after they left California, both men rode into Missouri on horseback pulling their five-mule caravan. Of course, the people on Dr. Bassett's plantation were glad to see them. But nobody was happier than Mrs. Coffey and her two young daughters when they saw Alvin Coffey ride into that plantation on a big, chestnut-brown stallion.

Coffey got up bright and early the next morning to do his normal chores around the plantation. Around noon, he took a break and walked to the main house. He noticed a horse and buggy tied up outside; inside, in the parlor, a rich-looking white fellow shook Dr. Bassett's hand. It seemed like the two of them were old friends. It occurred to Coffey that maybe this wasn't the right time to discuss his freedom with Dr. Bassett, but the closer he got to the house, the more he remembered old Jake and the others who had bought their freedom in California.

"Oh, that's you. Come on in," said Dr. Bassett, responding to Alvin Coffey's knock on the back door.

As Coffey walked into the parlor the rich-looking white man smiled at him.

"He's the one I told you about," Bassett said to the other white gentleman. "He's trustworthy, strong, and can do figures pretty good, and is very resourceful," bragged Dr. Bassett.

"I'm impressed. I think I cut a pretty good deal," the other white man said.

"Him and his family...a fine working unit," Bassett responded.

"I'll be by to collect them first thing in the morning," the stranger said. Coffey stood there like a block of stone, unable to move or say a word. He had been utterly betrayed.

In a daze, Coffey followed Dr. Bassett and the other white man out onto the veranda. After the other man left, Coffey turned to Dr. Bassett. "What you goin' to do about the money I gave you for my freedom?" he asked.

"Forget it," Bassett said. "That belongs to me anyway. You're my slave remember." Bassett turned on his heel to go back into the main house, adding over his shoulder, "Get all your things together by tomorrow at five-thirty. You and your family will be leaving with Mr. Stuart at the break of dawn.''

Coffey walked slowly back to the fields. He had begun to recover from the shock of what had just happened, and smiled grimly to himself. That night after dinner, his curious wife asked him, ''Well, you gonna tell me about California?''

''Woman,'' he said, ''California is so big, with giant mountains and sandy shores. The air there is so sweet you can open your mouth and take a bite out of it. You, me, and the girls are goin' to live there some day. But that day ain't now. I got somethin' to tell you . . .''

''What is it . . .'' Coffey's wife said with alarm. She saw how his mood had changed, and it frightened her.

''Well, there's two things: one good and the other bad,'' Coffey said. ''First the bad. I paid that low-down varmint Bassett seven hundred dollars as a down payment to buy our freedom. Now I find out the so-and-so done stole it from me. And on top of that, he sold us to another plantation owner. We movin' tomorrow mornin'.''

Coffey's wife sagged in her chair and let out a moan when she heard this.

''Now, now,'' Coffey said. ''I said there was the bad and the good. Let me show you the good.'' He reached into the saddlebag that contained his clothes, canteen, and mining pan from California. Out of it he pulled two gold nuggets, each one as big as a goose egg. ''Do you know what this is?'' he asked.

''I think so,'' she said as she wiped her tears from her eyes. She took it into her hands. The stones were heavy and dazzled her eyes. ''Why, Alvin . . .'' she said as her tears turned to a smile.

''Ummm huh . . .'' he said with a big smile on his face.

''I saved these just for us—they'll help us get to California, someday!''

Coffey and his family had worked for Mr. Stuart, their new master, almost a year. He noticed there was something different about this white man. Many times after all the chores were done, Mr. Stuart would call Coffey over to talk about California. At first Coffey thought the man wanted to just pick his brain for information to use against him in case he decided to run off. But eventually, when he sensed his new master was sincere, Coffey opened up more and more. One night they were talking when Mr. Stuart told Coffey something that took him by surprise. ''I remember the look in your eyes that day Bassett sold you to me. You looked like a man who just had the rug pulled out from under him. What happened?''

Coffey hesitated at first but he eventually told the story about the agreement he and Dr. Bassett had made between them when they were out in California. ''He lied to me. He took my money and never kept his word,'' said Coffey.

''That explains the look on your face. You probably think all white men are liars, don't you?'' asked Stuart. Coffey just looked at him without saying a word. ''I'm going to make an agreement with you, and I'll keep it, so help me God,'' Stuart said, looking Coffey right in the eyes. ''You go back to California and make me fifteen hundred dollars, and you will have earned your freedom. Include an additional seven hundred dollars apiece for your wife and children, and I'll send them to you. You have my word as a man of honor,'' he said, stretching forth his hand to shake the hand of Alvin Coffey.

Coffey was beside himself with joy. He had so much to tell his wife that night he could hardly speak. ''I don't know how long it's gonna take, but it shouldn't take too long, not with these little darlings to give me a head start," he said as he held up the two nuggets he had been hiding.

Three days later, Alvin Coffey kissed his family good-bye, and headed west with a pair of mules loaded down with supplies. This time he was older and more experienced when he arrived in San Francisco. The excitement of the gold rush had died down somewhat. The town was bigger now, and almost all of the tent cities were gone. Many of the streets had been paved with cobblestone. There was a big new opera house downtown, and across the street several fancy hotels catered to spiffed up businessmen and their ladies.

There was still gold up in the hills for a man determined enough to get at it. But as fortune would have it, Coffey reckoned he wouldn't have to work the fields quite as much this time around. He went directly to the gold assayers office and sold the two nuggets he had been keeping for himself and his family. The man behind the window just whistled when Coffey handed over the rocks. Coffey walked out of the office with a cool $2,000, a good start to getting his family back.

Coffey then proceeded to get himself a claim and went to work right away. He worked hard night and day. Six months later, his efforts were rewarded. He hit a gold vein that paid out. It wasn't one of those "big ones" that miners always dreamed of, but it was enough.

Within a week he sent $2,900 to Mr. Stuart back in Missouri, along with a note that he dictated. "God has smiled on me," the note said. "Have hit pay dirt. Please send Mrs. Coffey and young'uns along on next coach. Yours truly, Alvin Coffey."

Back then mail and money had to travel by stage coach, and depending on the route, it could take up to a month to get mail. From Missouri to San Francisco took about thirty days. Coffey didn't waste a minute of that time. He staked out some land he bought with his money and built a small house just big enough for his family. He figured with the rest of his money he could always build a bigger house.

On a fine autumn day in 1853, a stagecoach rumbled into San Francisco with three passengers. Standing on the platform to greet them with fresh daisies in his hand stood one proud man, Alvin Coffey. The door swung open and out stepped Mrs. Coffey followed by two pretty little girls.

"Alvin?" smiled his wife.

"Yes, ma'am," replied Coffey, and they hugged each other and cried.

"Daddy, me too," said his two little girls jumping up and down. He hugged all of them as if his life depended on it.

"Come on, we goin' home," he said as he walked them over to his horse and buggy. They rode out of San Francisco to their new home—one family, free at last.

By the 1860s Alvin Coffey was doing mighty fine. His daughters were in school, and his family lived in a prosperous section of San Francisco. He and his wife had learned to read and write. Coffey had used his money well and had all the comforts of life to prove it. Later on, he was surprised when an all-white social group called the Society of California Pioneers voted him in as a member. Alvin Coffey was the only black man ever voted into that society.

The Old Cowboy tapped on his pipe to clean out the ashes of the tobacco he had smoked while he told his story. It was mid-afternoon now, and the sky was completely clear.

"Sundown," the Old Cowboy said, "there were many black men who worked the gold mines back in the hey-day of Forty-Niners. Alvin Coffey wasn't the only black man who paid for his freedom

in gold. But as I reflect on that time in this country's history, there's something about Alvin Coffey that just stands out in my mind. He had a bulldog determination to win his freedom and a strong will that kept him at his business."

The Old Cowboy got up and walked in a circle around the rock against which he had been sitting. He looked up at the sky, examining it closely in every direction. Then he checked the contents of the tobacco pouch he kept in his shirt pocket.

"Nice day, ain't it, Sundown," he said. "I got enough smokes to last a while. I reckon we have time to sit here a spell longer."

BIDDY MASON, WOMAN PIONEER

"Sundown, *black people came to California in a variety of ways,"* the Old Cowboy said as he gazed out to the distant mountains. *"Some came on horseback, some on mules, and others in covered wagons. But one black lady arrived in a most unusual and roundabout fashion."*

Her name was Biddy Mason, and she began her journey way back down in Mississippi. Biddy was a slave owned by a Mormon couple named the Smiths.

Now, most Mormons were Northerners. See, the Mormons were a religious group founded in New York and Ohio in the 1830s. Because their beliefs were so different from most other Christian groups, the Mormons were hounded by many of their neighbors. Under the guidance of their leader, Brigham Young, the Mormons trekked out West to set down roots in a place they could call their own. In 1847, they ended up in the valley of the Great Salt Lake in the territory that later would become the state of Utah. Soon after, the Smiths of Mississippi and other southern Mormons heeded Brigham Young's call to come West.

There weren't a whole lot of Mormons in the South, but there were enough so that in 1851 a group of them got ready to make the long, hard journey from Mississippi to Utah. On the Smith's plantation, all hands had packed wagons and mules as the household made last minute preparations for the journey. Now they all tried to sleep as they waited out the last night before the beginning of the trip.

In the middle of the night, Biddy Mason and her daughters, and most of the other slaves at the Smith plantation, were awakened by a commotion that brought everybody to their feet. "Hush, now!" Biddy whispered as she and her three girls peered from a window of the slave quarters.

Mr. Smith and about fifteen rough-looking white men stood around John, one of Mr. Smith's slaves. "We caught him trying to escape," one of the men said. "My bet is he was trying to get to that secret hiding place where all of them other slaves been running to."

"What place?" shouted Mr. Smith.

"We can't rightly tell, but a whole bunch of plantation owners like yourself been losing slaves like water flowing through a sieve," said another.

"I think we ought to make an example out of him so you don't lose no more," said another white man.

Mr. Smith thought about it for a moment. In a few hours the sun would come up and his three hundred wagons would roll out for Utah.

"Well, what you want us to do with him? Teach him a lesson?" asked one of the slave catchers.

"Move away from the window, right now!" commanded Biddy Mason to her daughters. The girls knew something was going to happen that their mama didn't want them to see, and they obeyed without question.

The runaway slave stood proud and erect, his hands and feet bound in chains. The bloodhounds that had tracked him down idly wandered around him.

"Do whatever you want with him," said Mr. Smith, as he turned and slowly walked up the steps to his house.

"Start a fire, boys. We got work to do!" shouted one of the slave catchers. A weak smile sneaked across the man's face as he roughly moved the slave John to a nearby field.

Biddy had grown up on plantations and when she heard "fire" the blood boiled in her veins. The slave catchers were going to set fire to John until he burned to death. The message would be delivered in the morning for all the other slaves to see: a horrible death was the price you paid for freedom.

The memory of John's execution stayed with Biddy throughout the months-long journey to Utah. Biddy had been given the job of walking behind the wagon train and herding the cows. Because of this, she and her three daughters slept in the last wagon of the caravan. She did her job well, but the cry of freedom rang in her heart. She vowed that her children would never have to hear the sound of a tortured slave again. She would make her move to freedom one day, but the timing had to be right. All she could do now was wait.

The group arrived in the Salt Lake Valley in 1851, but by the following year the Smiths had decided to move yet again—this time to a small town in southern California called San Bernardino. The Mormon leaders had decided southern California was prime territory for another Mormon city, so they sent a group out there to colonize the area.

''Where we goin' now?'' asked Biddy's youngest daughter.

''I ain't heard nothin' yet,'' Biddy said. ''But when I do, I'll let y'all know. Now hush up.''

Early the next morning Biddy and her three daughters rose before the sun had a chance to blink. They weren't alone either; the other slaves belonging to Mr. Smith were already up doing their chores. Biddy was busy gathering the sheep when an older slave woman named Hannah carefully approached her. ''We ain't been here long and we moving out again. I hear master Smith say they suppose' to build a new church in California somewhere.''

''I hear the same as you, child. I guess we find out for sure when we get there,'' replied Biddy.

Biddy and Hannah both had family on the trip. Their daughters played together when they had time, but Biddy kept her feelings about things to herself. Whatever she and her daughters talked about didn't go further than the family. The sun was just where it ought to be around nine that morning, shining down through bright, fluffy white clouds scattered across a big, blue Utah sky.

''We're ready when you are, sir,'' said the wagonmaster.

Mr. Smith turned toward his wagon train, took a long look and was pleased with what he saw. ''Move 'em out,'' he said.

''Wagons ho!'' shouted the wagonmaster, and all three hundred ox-driven wagons and a herd of sheep pulled out. They were bound for California.

''Move it, you lazy varmints!'' shouted Biddy as her switch came down hard on the tail of an oxen.

''Mama, do they have cotton in California?'' asked Biddy's youngest daughter as she ran alongside her mother with a little switch, pretending to swing it at the oxen.

"I ain't never been in California. When we get there we'll see," said Biddy.

Her little girl was quiet for about a minute. "Mama, we gon' live in the master's house when we get to California?"

"I 'spect we might. That's decided by Master Smith. Why you asking 'bout cotton and where we gon' live?" asked Biddy as she slowed down her walking pace.

"Hannah say we got to pick cotton like we did back home, and that Master Smith ain't gon' let us live in no Big House with him and Missus Smith."

"How Hannah know what's in California? She ain't never been there. I doubt she can read the master's mind whether he gon' move us in his house or not. When we get to California, we will see what we will see. Now you go on back there and help your sister with them sheep. We ain't in California yet," said Biddy.

It was a long trip, but by the spring of 1852 the wagon train at last came to San Bernardino.

"My, my, my," Mr. Smith said as he stopped on a ridge outside of the city. "It's about the prettiest sight I ever seen." San Bernardino offered some of the most beautiful pastoral land he or any of the other Mormons had come across. Wild mustangs ran as free as a country breeze; herds of cattle roamed the plains and grazed like guests at a royal feast.

Mr. Smith and the other Mormons drove at the head of the wagon train into San Bernardino. Bringing up the rear was Biddy Mason, walking and driving the sheep. I suppose Hannah would have been walking right along with her, but she was pretty old and her job was to care for the children.

Since there were so many people in the wagon train, the wagonmaster had everybody camp outside of town, while he and Mr. Smith and some of the other men rode into San Bernardino. As the seat of county government, San Bernardino was the place where all the officials met and where the records were kept. The men rode to the county courthouse, where they intended to find out which land was for sale.

San Bernardino was a sleepy little town. It didn't have all the hustle and bustle of gold rush fever like San Francisco. San Bernardino didn't have very many black people, either. Counting those who arrived with the Mormons, there weren't more than seventeen black folks in the whole town.

"There it is over there," said Mr. Smith, pointing to the courthouse. He and the wagonmaster rode over, tied up their horses, and walked in. The county clerk eyed the two men carefully.

"Welcome, gentlemen, to San Bernardino," he said. "Y'all caused quite a commotion round here. It ain't every day we get visitors like you in these parts."

Mr. Smith figured as much. He knew the clerk pegged them as strangers by their dress as soon as they walked into the place. They were the first Mormons in southern California. People were likely to be curious.

"Y'all plan on staying long?" the clerk asked.

"That depends," Mr. Smith said. "We want to purchase land outside of town to build homes and do some farming."

"How many acres you willing to buy?" asked the clerk, looking over the top of his spectacles.

"Oh, I'd say about one hundred acres to start and more later," replied Mr. Smith.

"Well now, let's see what we can do..." said a very anxious county clerk.

I guess that clerk made the deal of his life. He got the

proper papers together real quick and by the time Mr. Smith and the wagonmaster walked out of there, everything was in order.

Mr. Smith rode back to the wagon train and broke the news to the others. They all rejoiced and jumped at the chance to start building a new settlement. Within a few weeks, you could see little houses sprouting up all around and oxen plowing the fields.

Biddy and her daughters were working as the personal slaves to the Smith family, and Mr. Smith saw to it that all her chores kept her close to the settlement. California was a free state, a state where slavery was legally forbidden, and Mr. Smith didn't want Biddy to find out about that.

By 1855 Biddy and her daughters and the few other slaves had been in San Bernardino for about three years. Mr. Smith had done a pretty good job of keeping her and the others ignorant about their freedom. All was going well until one day, when Mrs. Smith needed some dry goods and called Biddy to the house. "I know you can't read, Biddy, but I want you to take this note into town. Just ask somebody for the dry goods store, and they'll show you. You know how I love sugar with my tea. Well, we're out of sugar and I can't wait two days until Mr. Smith gets back before I have tea again."

Biddy went over to the stable and hitched up the buckboard wagon and a team of horses to go into town. "Mama, can I go with you?" asked her older daughter, who was starting to show all the signs of womanhood. Biddy paused for a minute, then thinking that she and her daughter might not get a chance like this again, she said, "Jump on board."

Neither one of them had ever been in that town, but Mrs. Smith gave her very good directions. It was a bright sunny day, and the two of them rode into San Bernardino right around lunch time. Only a few people milled about those dusty streets, but to Biddy and her daughter they were streets of dreams.

"Look, Mama, over there!" Biddy's daughter said. She pointed to a dress shop with dresses hanging in the window. "Let's go over there!"

"Hold your horses. We suppose' to find a dry goods store for the missus. She got to have her sugar," said Biddy. Biddy was trying to hold back her excitement. She hadn't seen much of anything on the plantation in Mississippi. Now she was looking at men and women dressed in fine clothes, buildings painted all white, and there were even wooden sidewalks for you to walk on.

As her eyes swallowed up as much as they could without giving her surprise away, she noticed a black man coming up to their wagon. He was dressed unlike any slave she had ever seen.

"You ladies look lost. Perhaps I can help you," he said.

Biddy's daughter looked at the young man with the strangest stare. "We want the dry goods store. Our master's wife wants five pounds of sugar," said Biddy, handing him the note.

He read the note. "I should be able to help you with this. My father owns a general store. Follow me."

You'd thought somebody had just put a spell on Biddy and her daughter as they followed this man over to his father's store. The young man's father smiled as he watched both ladies turn in more directions than a leaf in a hurricane.

"Father, will you fill this order for these two beautiful ladies," said the son, handing him the note.

"Five pounds of sugar. That's easy enough," the father said. "By the way, where are you ladies from?"

"We work for the Smith family outside of town," said Biddy.

"You mean that religious community... the Mormons, right?" the son asked.

"Yes," Biddy said.

"I know Mr. Smith. He comes in here often."

"That'll be fifty cents. I'll just add it to Mr. Smith's bill," said the father. The father looked at Biddy and her daughter very carefully before he asked the next question. "Does he pay you wages, ma'am?" he asked.

A puzzled look flashed across Biddy's face. "What be wages?" Biddy asked.

The father knew right then what was going on. "Did you come here as a slave?" he continued.

"All the way from Mississippi," replied Biddy's daughter. "How come y'all don't look like we do, and you own all this?" she continued.

"Because we are free," said the son. "California is a free state, but if you come here as a slave it can be dangerous getting your freedom unless you take your master to court, and in this town the judges rule on the side of the whites. Your only hope are the courts in Los Angeles," he continued.

It was getting late, and Biddy knew she had to get back with the sugar. All this talk about freedom and the courts was a mystery she had to think on, but now wasn't the time. "Come on, we best be gettin' back," she said to her daughter.

"Will you be coming to town again?" the son asked Biddy's daughter.

"I don't think so," interrupted Biddy, grabbing her daughter's arm as they hurried out from the store.

Images of black people owning businesses, walking

around free, played in Biddy's mind like the favorite hymn of a church choir. All her life, she and her daughters had worked for the Mormons. Before, their only hope of freedom lay in the unlikely chance that their masters would one day set them free. But now there was a chance that maybe the time of waiting was over. That ride back to the settlement seemed to last forever.

Several days later, Mr. Smith returned from his trip to Los Angeles. Biddy had cooked up a mess of pies, which she had placed along the window ledge to cool.

"I want you to be on your best behavior tonight," Mrs. Smith said to her husband. "We're having company. I've invited Mrs. Rowen from town. I met her at one of the sewing parties. I hope you don't mind."

Before Mr. Smith could say a word, Mrs. Rowen's carriage pulled up to the front door. "That must be her," Mrs. Smith said as she got up to greet their guest. One of the male slaves took the carriage and another escorted Mrs. Rowen to the front door.

"Come right on in," Mrs. Smith said.

As Mrs. Rowen entered the foyer, her eyes danced around the room. "What a beautiful home. You both must be very proud."

"Biddy keeps this place spotless," said Mr. Smith.

"Biddy? Who's Biddy?" asked Mrs. Rowen as Mrs. Smith led her into the sitting room.

"Biddy works for us. She's been in our family forever," continued Mrs. Smith.

Once they were seated Biddy brought them tea and shortbread cakes. "Dinner will be served shortly," she said.

"Thank goodness. I'm starving," replied Mr. Smith. "Biddy's one of the best cooks in these parts," he bragged to Mrs. Rowen.

"Judging from these teacakes," Mrs. Rowen said, "I'll have to agree."

Once dinner was over, everybody returned to the sitting room. Biddy was clearing the table when she overheard Mrs. Rowen. "That was the best pheasant I ever tasted. My compliments to your cook," she said.

"Out of all our slaves, Biddy is the best. She can outcook them all," Mr. Smith said, laughingly.

"Slaves did you say?"

"Well you know what I mean. She belongs to us, but we treat her like family."

"Don't you know it's against the law to hold slaves in the state of California?" said Mrs. Rowen, with a more serious tone to her voice. "If Biddy and your other slaves have not been set free since you all arrived here some three years ago, then you're in violation of California state law."

"Now, Mrs. Rowen, I'm sure if Biddy and the others wanted to be free, they would have left a long time ago," said Mr. Smith with some agitation. "But as you can see, she and the others are happy right where they are. Now I don't think we need to discuss this any further. It's getting late, and you have a long way to go back to town."

Mrs. Rowan knew she had hit a nerve. From the mirror hanging over the mantle, she saw Biddy staring at her. She was glad Biddy had overheard their conversation. "You're right. I should be going," she said as she stood up. "I surely appreciated your hospitality, and I do hope you allow me to extend an invitation for dinner at my house."

"I'm sure we'll look forward to that," said Mr. Smith, hurrying to get Mrs. Rowen's wrap.

Biddy was taking her good time clearing off the table. She looked into the mirror again, and to her surprise, she saw Mrs. Rowen staring right back at her, giving her a smile and a wink. Biddy got a warm feeling in the pit of her stomach. She knew she'd see this white woman again.

Mrs. Rowen had no sooner gotten out of sight, then Mr. Smith slammed the door. Turning to his wife, he yelled, "Don't ever invite anybody to this house from town again unless you tell me first. Is that clear?"

"I didn't know you would get so upset. What's the problem?" said a somewhat confused Mrs. Smith.

"I don't like that woman. All that talk about the law and setting my slaves free. She doesn't understand. These are my slaves, my property, and ain't no state law gonna change that!"

"Will that be all for tonight?" asked Biddy, standing in the doorway of the kitchen.

"How long you been standing there?" asked Mr. Smith, thinking that she might have heard his conversation.

"I just walked up, sir," Biddy said. "I just finished feeding my children. When the lady rode off, I figured I'd see if y'all needed anything."

"Don't mind Mr. Smith, Biddy," said Mrs. Smith. "He's just a little tired. We won't be needing anything else tonight. Finish cleaning up and you can leave."

"Yes, ma'am," said Biddy as she turned and went back into the kitchen.

Riding home that night, Mrs. Rowen knew she and Biddy had made a connection. When Biddy smiled back at her from the mirror that was all the encouragement she needed to make her next move. She knew from her instincts that she had made Mr. Smith very nervous. A nervous man was like a wild mustang; he's liable to do anything. Mrs. Rowen didn't have a whole lot of time. She had helped other slaves like Biddy, whose masters refused to free them once

they arrived in California. Her only hope to free Biddy was to get word to the Los Angeles sheriff. Once the slaves were in his protection, they would plead their case before a judge in the Los Angeles courts.

Biddy couldn't sleep a wink that night. She kept what happened in the Smith's house to herself. There was something truly genuine in the smile of that white lady. Even though the two of them never met, she too got the feeling that they had made a connection. But that moment of joy was quickly followed by sorrow. She had heard every bit of Mr. Smith's conversation. She also knew he was very angry at Mrs. Rowen for telling him about the law and advising him to set his slaves free. Biddy feared he might do something desperate to keep her and the other slaves forever.

The next morning Mrs. Smith called Biddy into the house. "Biddy, I want you to get the others together and start packing. My husband had a vision last night and fears that evil has spread throughout our settlement. So we must depart from here and go to Texas where we'll all be safe. I want you to have things ready by the end of the week." When she heard this, Biddy became alarmed. She'd overheard some of the other Mormons talk about Texas and how slaves were treated. If Mr. Smith took her away from California, she was afraid that she and her children would never be free.

Mrs. Rowen hadn't wasted a minute. The very next morning she hitched up her wagon and rode to nearby Los Angeles to report directly to the local sheriff.

"Yes, ma'am!" said the sheriff, taking his feet off his desk in a hurry. "What can I do for you?"

"I'm here on a matter of great concern, and I want immediate action!" said Mrs. Rowen.

"Just what is the problem?"

"There are slaves being held against their will by a family of Mormons in San Bernardino. You know California is a free state and to hold slaves is against the law," she said.

"Are you sure they're being held against their will?" he asked.

"I'd bet my life on it! We don't have much time. My instincts tell me if we don't move quickly those poor souls will be in great danger."

"This is going to take a few days getting the papers drawn up for a warrant . . ."

"We don't have days, sheriff. Every minute is precious," she said.

The sheriff knew this woman meant business, and he wasn't about to disappoint her. "Okay I'll go stir up Judge Hayes and see what I can do for you," he said.

Biddy and the other slaves were busy packing and preparing to move on to Texas. Each day she'd look out to see if a stranger was coming up the road, but each day it was the same—no one.

"We should be ready to go by tomorrow," said Mrs. Smith.

"Good," Mr. Smith said. "I don't want to waste any-more time. I've got the name of a fella who says he can get us a nice piece of land in Texas. So we can make a new start."

By the end of the week, all was in order. The wagons were full; the cattle were ready to go; and Mr. Smith had his slaves—all fourteen of them—ready to march. Mrs. Smith took a last, loving look at her home. Her daydream was broken by the harsh sound of her husband's voice. "Move out!" he said, as he cracked a whip over the oxen's heads.

It took longer than both Mrs. Rowen and the sheriff figured but finally they managed to get a warrant from the judge. With the warrant in his pocket, the sheriff spurred a fast stallion, and was off to San Bernardino like a bullet shot from a Winchester rifle. Roaring into the Mormon settlement like a Texas tornado, the sheriff sought out the first person he saw.

"Can I help you, sheriff?" one of the Mormons asked.

"I'm looking for a Mr. Robert Smith."

"You missed him by three days. They moved on to Texas," he said.

"You know which way they went?"

"No, I don't reckon I do," the Mormon said suspiciously.

"I see. Well thank you so much for your help," the sheriff said. The sheriff knew the man was lying, but that didn't matter. He was confident that he could track the trail of the Smith party. It was a large group, with a number of wagons and cattle. He rode out to the Smith ranch, and sure enough, like a big, ol' road sign, a rutted trail led southeast toward Yuma. Now he had to ride hard if he was going to catch them before they made it to the Arizona border.

Mr. Smith pushed his group hard the first three or four days. He wanted to move his party quickly out of the San Bernardino area and march across the desert to Yuma. From there he would cross the border either into Arizona or Mexico and head east to Texas. Once he was across the Mexican border, he would be safe. American slaveholders weren't bothered in Mexico, and slavery had not yet been outlawed in Arizona Territory.

The Smith group approached the outskirts of Yuma on their sixth day out of San Bernardino. By now, cattle and men were thoroughly exhausted from their grueling trek across the desert. Smith and his party pulled up to a cozy spot on the Colorado River and staked out a campsite.

"We'll stay here a few days and rest up before moving on," said a cocky Mr. Smith. The fear of losing his slaves was replaced by a bold confidence.

Biddy Mason, however, didn't feel so chipper. She stared sadly out at the swift waters of the Colorado River.

"What we goin' to do?" her oldest daughter asked. "I heard from one of the white men that once we on the other side of that river, ain't no man can set us free."

"That seems to be right, child," Biddy said.

Both mother and daughter lapsed into silence. After a while Biddy spoke. "I want you and the other girls to be real quiet like and gather up a few things in a knapsack. Later on tonight, we goin' to go hide in the desert. I don't see that we got any other choice."

"But what Mr. Smith do if he catch us?" the daughter asked.

The horrible memory of the killing of the slave John passed in front of Biddy's eyes. She took her daughter to her and held her closely. "Ain't nothing going to happen, child. We just can't go on like this anymore."

By sundown, Biddy and her family were ready to leave camp. They waited for things to quiet down so they could slip away unnoticed. Mr. Smith had ordered the other Mormons to inspect and clean their firearms, so many of the men were doing this as the sun began to go down over the mountains to the west. Suddenly, one of the Mormons noticed a cloud of dust in the distance. It got larger and larger, indicating that a man or men were nearing the camp.

"Ready your arms, men," Mr. Smith cried.

Out in the desert in those days, you never knew who you might encounter, and the Mormons took no chances. As the dust cloud got closer, the Mormons saw that it was just a party of three white men.

"At ease," Mr. Smith said, and everyone relaxed, figuring the men were just a bunch of crazy cowboys out for a joy ride.

The sheriff and two of his deputies blew into the Smith camp like a Cheyenne war party.

"I'm looking for Mr. Robert Smith," the sheriff demanded as he dismounted his horse in a cloud of dust.

"I'm Mr. Smith. What's the trouble?"

Biddy and the other slaves had gathered around the wagons. They looked on with deep concern.

"Mr. Smith, you are authorized to appear in the Los Angeles court. A legal petition has been filed against you by the state of California for holding slaves. I am hereby authorized to hold them in my custody until a hearing is called. This will probably happen within three days of our return to Los Angeles. Here's the writ signed by the Honorable Judge Benjamin Hayes."

Mr. Smith stood there like a man struck dumb, holding the writ in his hand.

"I want all of you to get into a few wagons and follow me back to Los Angeles," said the sheriff to Biddy and the others. Turning to Mr. Smith, he said, "You'll get your wagons back after the hearing."

A week later, Biddy and the other slaves were brought to Judge Hayes' court.

"All rise," said the bailiff.

"The Honorable Judge Benjamin Hayes." Everybody stood. The judge entered the courtroom.

"Please be seated," said the bailiff. On the left side of the aisle, seated at the front row, were Biddy, her three daughters, Hannah, and her grandchildren, and the other slaves. Mr. Smith, his wife, and a few Mormons sat on the right side. At the back of the courtroom sat Mrs. Rowen.

"This court will come to order," said the judge. Looking at his papers, he said, "We have a petition filed against Mr. Robert Smith by Biddy, saying that she and her family and other persons are being held against their will as slaves. How do you plead Mr. Smith?"

Standing, Mr. Smith said, "I'm not guilty, your Honor."

"Perhaps you can explain how Biddy, her children, and the others came under your supervision," continued the judge.

"I'll do my best. See, your Honor, as you know in Mississippi it ain't a crime to hold slaves. Biddy, her children, and Hannah have been my property since I can remember."

"You're in the state of California now," said the judge. "We have laws against keeping people as slaves."

"Now hold on, your Honor. We both know that white men right here in Los Angeles have slaves. I ain't doing nothing they ain't doing already," said a riled up Mr. Smith.

"If their slaves bring a petition against them like yours did against you, I'd hear their case," replied the judge. Benjamin Hayes had come from Missouri and knew all about slavery. He also hated everything it stood for. He had tried two cases just like this one before and each time he set the slaves free.

Trying to find some sign of weakness that he could use to make his case stronger, Mr. Smith looked over at Biddy and Hannah. When he stared at Hannah she lowered her head. A sly smile crept across his lips. Changing his tone of voice, he said, "Your Honor, if the court will forgive my previous behavior, I'd like to just ask the court one thing.''

''Go right ahead, ask your question,'' said the judge.

''If I understand the California law correctly, my slaves can decide to work for me of their own free will?''

''If they want to work for you of their own free will and you pay them, I see no harm in that arrangement,'' said the judge.

''Then, your Honor, do you mind if I ask them that question?''

''I have no objection,'' said the judge.

What Mr. Smith wanted to do was to ask Hannah, the oldest, that question, figuring her answer would sway the judge into believing she and Biddy really didn't want to be free. Turning to Hannah, Smith asked, ''Hannah you've been with me and my family for a long time haven't you?''

''Yes, sir,'' Hannah mumbled.

''Haven't we always taken care of you and your family?''

''Yes, sir, Master Smith.''

Biddy sat next to Hannah and she could see what Smith was up to. Mrs. Rowen, at the back of the courtroom, now sat on the edge of her seat. She knew if Biddy and her family were to go free, they all had to show unity and right now Hannah was starting to crumble. Hannah couldn't look at Biddy. She was scared; she had been a slave too long.

''Hannah, have I or my wife ever mistreated you or spoken unkindly to you?'' Smith asked.

Hannah was shaking now. ''No, master,'' she replied.

''Don't you feel at home with my wife and myself?'' Smith continued.

Hannah turned and glanced in Biddy's direction. Biddy's stare was as fiery as a whitehot branding iron. ''I don't rightly know, sir,'' mumbled Hannah.

''Let me put it another way, Hannah. Don't you want to

live where you will be taken care of for the rest of your natural life?''

Before Hannah could answer, Biddy stood up and spoke. ''Your Honor, may I say something?''

''Yes,'' the judge said.

''Your Honor, I been a slave all my life. I seen men beaten with whips so bad, their backs were laid open like ripe melons. I seen women who just give birth to their babies, have them snatched from their bosoms and the women made to go right back in the field and pick cotton.'' Looking in Mr. Smith's direction. ''I seen a grown man burned up like kindlin' cause he ran off lookin' for his freedom. I can't speak for Hannah and her children, but I sho' can speak for my family. We don't need nobody to take care of us. I been takin' care of white folks all my life. All I need is my freedom, and I can take care of my family. Your Honor, you sound like a god fearin' man. Down deep in your bones, you know it just ain't right for me and my family to be slaves to nobody. Now I done said my piece.'' Biddy took her seat and Mrs. Rowen sat back on her bench, feeling a whole lot better.

''I think I've heard from everybody. Do you have anything else to say Mr. Smith?'' asked the judge.

''No, your Honor,'' he said.

''Good, this court finds that the freedom of Biddy, her daughters, Hannah, and her family, and the others has been violated, and it is my judgement that both families in this matter be set free.''

''Praise the Lord!'' shouted Biddy as she cried and hugged her family.

''We free Mama?'' cried her youngest daughter.

''Yes, child, we is free!'' cried Biddy.

During all the excitement Mr. Smith and his wife hurried

from the courtroom, bumping into Mrs. Rowen on their
way out. Stopping for a quick moment, Mr. Smith looked
Mrs. Rowen square in the eyes. She didn't turn her head one
bit, but stared him right back in his face. He brushed by her
like a fast wind, boarded his wagon and headed onto Texas.

Biddy pulled herself away from her family when she saw
Mrs. Rowen standing by the doorway. "I want to thank
you, Ma'am. I don't even know your name," said Biddy.

"I'm Mrs. Rowen, a friend," she said.

"When I saw you that night at supper, and you winked at
me in the mirror, I figured the lord sent you. I'm mighty
grateful, and may you be blessed," said Biddy.

For the next ten years Biddy worked hard as a midwife and
a nurse, saving every penny she earned. She took a full name,
Biddy Mason. I'm not sure where she got her last name, but
it stuck with her until she died. It wasn't long before Biddy
started to use her money wisely. She bought one piece of
land in Los Angeles, then another and another. Los Angeles
was growing, but it was still mostly made up of large
stretches of grassy land filled with cattle ranches and
vaqueros—Spanish cowboys.

Not much was heard of Hannah after that day in court. I
suspect she made a life for herself, but Biddy Mason wasted
no time making up for her lost freedom. Her daughters all
grew up and got their schooling and married smart men so I
hear.

By 1866, according to town records, only eighty-seven
black people, including Biddy Mason and her family, lived in
Los Angeles. Biddy's family had grown by then. She had
become a proud grandmother. When the land boom hit Los
Angeles in the late 1860s, she sold for $200,000 a piece of
land she had bought for $250. Now she was a very rich and

powerful woman, but the only thing that was larger than her money was her heart. She built schools for children and helped the sick and the needy. If you were a stranger in town and missing a hot meal and a place to stay, Biddy's home was always open. And another thing that made her special was that her doors were open to Mexicans, blacks, and white folks. If you were in need, Biddy was there, lending a helping hand.

On a warm summer day in 1891 Biddy rocked in her favorite chair on the big front porch of her home, humming to herself.

"Grandma, did you really walk all the way from Mississippi to California like my Mama said?" asked her grandson.

Biddy looked at him and smiled, "I sho' did."

"Didn't your feet hurt when you got to California?" Biddy didn't answer. She slumped in her chair as though she was asleep. "Grandma, grandma!" her grandson said, shaking Biddy's arm. "Wake up, grandma!" he shouted.

Biddy couldn't hear him. The lord had given her new "walking shoes" and she was heaven bound. They buried Biddy Mason later that week. Nearly all of Los Angeles showed at the funeral to remember Biddy. She had been a thirty-two year old slave when she walked into California in 1852, and thirty-nine years later she died a wealthy woman. But best of all, she used her freedom to serve her fellow man.

It was getting late in the afternoon, and a storm was gathering in the mountains to the west. The Old Cowboy got up and stretched his legs.

"I often wonder if one of the reasons Biddy Mason treated white folks kindly had anything to do with Mrs. Rowen and that no-nonsense judge Benjamin Hayes. What do you think, Sundown?"

Sundown yawned and yipped, and looked up at the Old Cowboy expectantly.

"Well, come on now. We'd best be goin' if we don't want to get drenched." The mongrel followed him through the knee-high grass, and in a short while they disappeared down the trail that led into the forest.

GEORGE MONROE AND THE RIDERS OF THE PONY EXPRESS

"Sundown, the year 1860 marked a short but glorious moment in our nation's history. Sometime around five o'clock in the afternoon of April 3, 1860, the first rider of the Pony Express mounted a half-breed California mustang in St. Joseph, Missouri, and galloped off to deliver the mail."*

You see, before 1860 there just weren't very many ways to bring mail rapidly between the East and West Coasts of the United States. And it didn't move very fast either if you happened to be stuck at a lot of places in-between. Before 1859, there just wasn't any rail service west of the Missouri River. A letter, for instance, from someone in San Francisco to kinfolks in Georgia, New York, or Virginia took a full eight months or more to be delivered by the Pacific Mail Steam Ship Company's route around Cape Horn at the tip of South America. Or you could send the letter by way of the Overland Mail Company stagecoach, which traveled from San Francisco to St. Joseph, Missouri, where the rail lines began. This route took twenty days and was the fastest delivery service available.

Now, a lot of politicians, especially ones from California, were upset with this state of affairs. One of the most hard-driving of these men was Senator William Gwin of California. To try to create a new, fast mail service between his state and the rest of the nation, Senator Gwin met in 1859 with Mr. William Russell, one of the owners of Russell, Majors, and Waddell, a company that specialized in long-distance coach and hauling services in the West.

"Look here, Mr. Russell," said Senator Gwin. "The people of my state are hollering for something to be done to speed up the delivery of mail. I think the folks at your company are the people for the job. I'd like you to give top priority to a fast mail service."

"Well, senator," answered Mr. Russell. "I'd love to, but I can't make that decision alone. I have to discuss this with my two other partners." Russell gave the senator a big smile and pretended to be pleased with this new business opportunity. Actually, he was far from happy. A fast mail service was expensive. His company would have to set up an elaborate relay system between St. Joseph and San Francisco, hire hundreds of riders and keep a pool of thousands of horses in order to deliver mail in ten rather than twenty days overland.

Russell met with his partners to discuss the offer.

"Frankly, I think it's an exciting proposition," said

Waddell. "Think of it—young riders galloping at lightning speed across this great land of ours, delivering mail with our company's name stamped on it. This could make us famous. We even have a chance to make history."

"Alright, then," said Russell at last. "We'll do it. But we'll need fast horses."

"Fast horses should be no problem," Colonel Majors said. The colonel was an old cavalry man and knew a thing or two about horses. "We can use California cayuses, mustangs, and ponies."

"That's it! That's it!" Waddell said.

The other two looked at him curiously. "What's it?" the colonel said at last.

"Look, we need a catchy name, something that will grab a hold of the public. We'll put the word out that this enterprise will be called the Pony Express!"

"Now that has a ring," chuckled the colonel.

The plan they devised to move the mail was simple, yet depended on clockwork execution. Mail traveled from New York to St. Joseph, Missouri, by railroad. From there it was placed on a steamboat and crossed the Missouri River. At this point, the Pony Express, covering a route of over two thousand miles of wild and untamed country, took over. A fresh rider picked up the mail and took off cross country toward California. Each rider rode a sixty to seventy mile run, stopping at relay stations long enough to change horses. When the rider completed his run, a fresh rider would take the mail from him and continue for another seventy miles or so, then pass the mail to yet another rider until the mail reached California. The Pony Express worked the same way going from California to Missouri.

Choosing Pony Express riders was no easy job. The men

had to know how to ride, shoot, speak several Indian tongues, but most of all, they had to be slender in body type and strong as a bull. Few men could fit the bill, but a handful made the cut. The one who stands out the most in my mind was a black man named George Monroe.

Monroe was the son of a gold miner during the heyday of California's gold rush. He was perfectly made for the role of a Pony Express rider. Not only did he have the body type for that job, but George could handle a horse like he was born on it.

One of the men doing the hiring for the Pony Express was Bolivar Roberts, manager of the western half of the business. One day early in 1860, he rode into Carson City, Nevada, looking for men to hire. When word leaked out that Roberts was in town, young men grabbed their fastest ponies and headed there quicker than a squirrel can blink. Among them was George Monroe.

"I hear they payin' pretty good wages for this new job," said one would-be rider to another.

"Anything's better than what I got right now, which is a pocketful of nothing," laughed another. All the men had gathered over at the livery stable waiting for Mr. Roberts to show up. George rode up in a cloud of dust and dismounted with the ease and style of a showman. The other men took notice of how George handled his horse with so much confidence and skill.

Around ten in the morning, Mr. Roberts finally made his way over to the livery stable to check out what kind of men answered his newspaper ad. As he got closer to the livery stable he saw old men, fat men, young boys, and young men, all of them as anxious as a bunch of corralled mustangs. He knew from a glance that he'd turn down most of them. He wasted no time in sorting out the men he thought had a chance at being hired. "You, you, and you stand over there. I'm sorry, son, you're too young. I can't use you either, sir," said Mr. Roberts as he picked his way through the crowd like a cowboy looking for the right saddle horse.

"You, mister, over there," Roberts said to George Monroe. The big foreman pointed toward the small cluster of men who had been chosen in the first round.

Once his first cut was selected, Roberts had to determine which of the chosen could ride and handle a horse. Now you got to understand, most men back in them days could ride a horse. If you couldn't you didn't get around much, but there were a few men that had a gift for riding and could make a horse do anything. Mr. Roberts knew the kind of territory these men would be riding through. Horsemanship would be key to their survival, especially in hostile Indian country.

Approaching the chosen few, Roberts said, "Men, as you know, you have been selected to compete for the jobs as riders with the Pony Express, but before you're hired you've got to show me you can handle a horse." By now the back of the livery was cleared out except for a few half-wild mustangs. Mr. Roberts had seen to it that these horses would be made ready just for this occasion. Once the men had gathered around back, each one was given a number. "Alright men listen up. When your number is called, I want you to grab a saddle over there on the fence, run over and saddle one of those Mustangs, and ride him around those three barrels and back to this finish line. You all got that?"

All the men mumbled they understood. George was the third man in line. He knew if he got the job it meant money in his empty pockets. He liked that, and he also liked the danger and prestige of being a Pony Express rider.

"I'm gonna nail this job down tighter than an under-taker's coffin," smiled a young cowboy to George.

George just smiled back. "Good luck fella," he said.

That cowboy's number was called, and he took off like a mule stung by a yellow jacket. He wasn't bad either. Fact was, he did a better than average job. Half out of breath, he charged across the finish line.

"Top that!" he said to George.

George just winked at the young fellow and when his number was called he was off to the races. He ran to his horse and had just got the saddle on when the mustang bolted and took off in a quick gallop. George had always been known to be quick and nimble as a deer and his speed served him well in this instance. Running alongside that stallion, he caught up with him and in one motion leaped up onto him, grabbing the horn of the saddle with one hand as his foot fit perfectly in the stirrup. Fast as greased lightning, he was on that stallion's back spinning him around like a tornado, heading him straight for the barrels. George moved past those barrels with such speed and ease, it was like watching a child play with his favorite toy. He turned a possible embarrassment into a skilled ride, and he did it in record time.

When he finished his ride, Mr. Roberts was anxious to see what the others could do, and he wasn't disappointed. Seems like George's little incident challenged the other cowboy's skills, and some of them started showing off. By the end of the day he had seen enough. He was pleased with his choices, and it was time to tell the men what they were hired for. "I'm pleased to say, all sixty of you men have been hired as riders for the Pony Express. What I'm about to tell you now may change your mind about working for us. Your pay will be $120 to $125 a month. You'll have to ride both day and night, in rain, snow, sleet. Nothing gentlemen, I mean nothing, will stop you from reaching your destination short of death. You'll encounter desperadoes, hostile Indians, and sometimes you'll have to ride double duty. Whatever is expected of you, you'll do. Your main objective is to get the letters through. Is that understood? Now how many still want the job?''

Not a single man backed away.

''Welcome aboard gentlemen. In the morning you'll be leaving for your first assignment.''

That was the beginning of man and a fast horse racing across this country to carry mail. Not only did these fellows have to be better than the average cowboy, but they also had to abide by a strict moral code. Those were the rules of the Pony Express.

One of the riders hired that day along with George Monroe was a white fellow named Jim Moore. Jim was one of the early Pony Express riders who set a standard that was hard to beat. He had the perfect body size, standing just shy of six feet, weighing about 160 pounds, small in the waist and broad in shoulders. According to those who knew him he could run like a panther and had more courage than a lion.

He must have looked a sight, too, in his buckskin pants and shirt, holstered Colt 45, and Bowie knife. You see, these Pony Express riders had a sort of unofficial uniform that distinguished them from other cowboys. Besides the buckskin duds, they also favored a hat with the front brim folded back so that the wind wouldn't blow it off, and they carried the letters wrapped in oil skins placed in a soft leather pouch that was strapped to the saddle.

Jim worked out of the Midway Station, which was

halfway between Fort Kearny and Julesburg, Colorado, a distance of about 140 miles. Jim's job was to ride his seventy miles, stopping at relay stations along the way to change horses. When he finished his stretch at the final station, he was met by a rider who took the mail from him and continued on while he rested a day or two. Then, a few days later, he started the route all over again. Like other riders, Jim let out a "coyote yell" when he got close to his final destination. That yell meant everyone had to be ready to take the mail pouch and hit the road.

"I guess I'll see you sometime tomorrow," said the station agent to Jim as he mounted up.

"I reckon so. When I get to Julesburg I'm gonna get me some shut-eye," replied Jim as he galloped off. He rode like a man on a mission, stopping every ten miles at a relay station to change horses and keep on going.

Every rider traveling his route got to know his route partner. It was necessary to be a good judge of character when it came to knowing the fellow that had to pick up where you left off. A fellow named Billy was Jim's route partner. Billy was black, but that didn't bother Jim any. The more he got to know Billy, the more Jim respected him.

"How do you do it Jim—riding day after day and not getting tired?" asked Billy.

Laughing, Jim said, "I guess it's in my blood. As a young boy I used to run with the Indians. We'd chase each other all up and down these Nebraska hills. I ran and ran and didn't rest 'til they did."

"Indians, huh?" Billy said with a frown on his face. "Indians were the ones who gave me this." He untied his buckskin shirt and showed Jim a recent, partially healed knife wound on his upper chest.

"You'd better take some time off, Billy," Jim said as he

examined the wound. "This looks pretty bad. If you don't take care of it, it'll get infected. Are you sure you can ride?"

Billy was a stubborn cuss. "Sure, I can ride," he said. "Besides, I ain't letting you beat me out of no week's worth of pay."

Jim laughed. "Ain't nobody gonna beat you out of no kind of money, but I'd have the doc look at it if I was you."

"Sure," Billy replied. "I'm gon' have the doc check it out when I ride out of here in the morning."

But Jim wasn't so certain about that. He had got to know Billy well, and Billy sure didn't like doctors.

Galloping lickkity split across the plains a week later Jim ran that conversation over and over in his mind like a tune stuck on a saloon piano. If you didn't have a strong body, riding like they did would wear a healthy man down after a while. Jim hoped that his partner had gone to the doctor like he said.

Jim's concern about Billy lingered in his mind all the way to Fort Kearny, Nebraska. He was riding hard and fast, thinking how if his partner was in bad shape, he would have to make up the lost time.

"Get it, boy!" Jim hollered and his horse jumped a little faster. As he came close to the relay station, Jim gave a coyote yell. No one answered so Jim dismounted and found a delirious Billy tossing and turning in his bed.

"You alright?" shouted Jim as he hurried over to his ailing friend.

"I'm sick. I think I got the fever," Billy whispered.

Jim had been hoping on getting a little rest. Since it was his final stop, he knew a rested Pony rider would be there in a minute to pick up his mail and carry it westward. Billy lay there sick with mail to be delivered east, where Jim had just left. The mail had to be delivered on time, which meant only one thing: Jim had to double back, right away. Cradling the head of his sick friend in his lap, Jim spoke softly, "Don't you fret none. Rest now. I'll get word to doc as quick as I can. Just take it easy." He laid Billy's head down gently, grabbed some cold meat and stuffed it in his pockets, downed a swag of coffee just in time to hear the "coyote yell." Taking one last look at his friend, Jim saw it was too late for doc. Billy had stopped struggling. He lay still now in the bed. Jim walked over and closed Billy's eyelids.

"What happened here," said a surprised Pony rider as he entered the relay station.

Wiping a little water from his eyes, Jim said, "Bury him. He's one of our own. I'll take his ride." With those words ringing in his ears like church bells on Christmas day, Jim grabbed Billy's horse, took the mail pouch, and like lightning shooting out of a thunder bolt, headed back to Julesburg, 70 miles away. In order to make up for lost time, Jim pushed that mustang for all he was worth. He rode into Midway one tired and sad man. He had covered 140 miles in just twenty-two hours from the time he left, but all he could think about was his friend Billy, who he would never see again.

During the time Jim Moore was cutting a swath through Nebraska and Colorado, George Monroe was busy making a name for himself in California. Moore's route ran between Merced and Mariposa, a distance of 140 miles. George was the fastest rider running this trail; nobody could match his time.

One day, the stationmaster called him aside, for a serious conversation. "George, come over here. I want to talk to you in private," said the stationmaster. "You know we lost two riders last week—MacDermot and Casey. Next to you they were two of my best riders. We been having trouble with desperadoes. The fools think we're carrying land claims and gold, when all we usually handle are business letters and government documents. Well, this time I've got a dispatch that really is important. You know about the Edmonds brothers?''

George shook his head yes. He knew how dangerous they were.

''I've got a judge's order that has to reach the Mariposa sheriff's office in seventeen hours,'' the stationmaster continued, ''so Johnny Edmonds can stand trial here in Merced for the murder of a bank teller he killed in a holdup. The sheriff can't hold him longer than that without this judge's order. If you don't make it in time, he'll go free and is liable to kill again. We got a little problem here, George. Johnny's brothers Will and Amos are out there waiting to catch this piece of paper. They know about the judge's order, I'm pretty sure that's why we lost MacDermot and Casey. If they stop this dispatch, Will knows his brother can go free. You don't have to take this ride, but you're the best man I've got. If you decide to go, you got to make it there before sundown tomorrow.''

George thought about it for a minute, but like I said earlier, a bit of danger attracted him like a moth to candlelight. ''When do I ride?'' George asked.

''Saddle up now,'' the stationmaster said.

George went to the stables and picked out a horse named Cheyenne that other riders refused to ride. That horse still had a lot of wild in him, but George figured if desperadoes were going to chase him, he needed the fastest hooves in the forest.

''Here's the dispatch and godspeed,'' said the stationmaster. George saddled up and shot out of Merced like a chicken running from a hungry fox.

Mariposa was 140 scary miles away, but danger was nothing to George. He had galloped through Indian country with no problems. No outlaws were going to bring him down either. Nothing at all happened the first hour or so, and he began to think the stationmaster was being maybe too careful. Twenty-five miles from Mariposa, though, things got pretty interesting. George rode through high mountain country now. He figured if anything was going to happen it would happen there. Of course, it could be that the Edmonds gang had given up trying to stop Pony riders, but deep down all the way to the soles of his cowboy boots, George felt that the Edmonds were waiting for him. ''Come on Cheyenne,'' he said as he gave the horse a little more leather.

''Well, looka here, boys,'' Amos Edmonds said. ''I think our waiting wasn't in vain.'' Amos peeked out from behind a boulder and watched George approach.

''I'll be darned. That old boy in the saloon back in Merced was tellin' the truth. He said it would probably be a black rider this time. Looks like we got ourselves another turkey shoot,'' said Will.

''Mount up. Johnny ain't got long. If that rider's carrying the judge's order for him to stand trial in Merced, he'll hang for sure. Now, let's get!'' Amos shouted. Like bats leaving a cave, the Edmonds gang swooped down on George.

George looked to his left and low and behold, he saw ten men riding hell-bent in his direction. So far he was out of gunfire range, but they were gaining on him. ''Come on boy, get it!'' George shouted. Like a steam-driven locomotive, Cheyenne jumped into a faster speed and left that gang farther behind.

They rode through canyons and across flat plains, but the Edmonds gang stayed on his trail like a hound dog on the scent of his favorite bone. After a while, Cheyenne slowed down and the Edmonds seemed to come closer and closer with each gallop. George knew he had run his horse long and hard, but he also knew mustang half-breeds could take a long race. He decided to play a little trick on this band of outlaws. Slowing down a bit, he let them get within gunfire range and sure enough they started firing away. Now George could shoot the eye out of a squirrel at fifty paces, with either hand. What those outlaws forgot was that their horses were tired, too. But unlike a pony rider's horse, a regular horse can't keep up over the long haul. The bullets whizzed past George's head. A couple of them came so close they practically gave him a shave. Turning in his saddle while galloping, George held the reins steadily in one hand as he turned and fired. He squeezed off three shots and three outlaws bit the dust. One of the outlaws spurred his horse and charged to about a horse's length from George, but George kicked Cheyenne and left that outlaw in a whirlwind of dust. When he looked back, all he could see was a speck of dust picked up by the outlaw's tired horse.

George paced Cheyenne steadily, now. The sun was setting, and he was running out of time. The stationmaster reminded him that he had to get to Mariposa before sunset. From a mile away, he could see the pony station. George rode in with a cloud of dust at his heels, and the stationmaster ran out to greet him. "You from Merced?" he shouted.

"Yes, sir," replied George.

"Give me that pouch!" he said.

George threw him the pouch and the stationmaster ran

over to the sheriff's office. "Sheriff, here it is," said the agent, gasping for breath.

Sheriff Daley ripped opened the envelope and read the judge's order. Looking Johnny Edmonds in the eye, he said, "Seems like you're gonna swing after all, Johnny. Thanks to that Pony Express rider."

All through 1860 and well into 1861, the Pony Express did a riproaring business carrying mail from California to Missouri and points in between. But during this nearly two-year period Misters Russell, Waddell, and Majors knew their company was battling time. See, they were facing tough competition. During this time, another company was building a transcontinental telegraph line across the West that eventually would link up California with the East Coast of the United States. The transcontinental telegraph could carry messages at the speed of light—one heck of a lot faster than any horse. Relentlessly, wooden telegraph poles were laid into the ground on a westward route. Month after month, reports flowed into Pony Express headquarters about the progress of the telegraph line. Finally, one day Russell came into the Pony Express conference room.

"What did I tell you, gentlemen," Russell said to Waddell and Majors. "Read this!" Russell held up a bulletin in big, bold print: "Transcontinental telegraph finally complete west of the Missouri."

Waddell sunk into his chair. "Well, it was bound to happen sooner or later."

"We can't compete with a telegraph system," Majors said.

"It's just as well," mused Waddell. "We're going broke anyway trying to keep all those relay stations open. Now we can cut our losses and get out of this business."

"Well, now, gentlemen," Russell said. "It's not all so bad. For a brief moment in history we were glorious."

"Glorious and broke," moaned Colonel Majors.

By October 7, 1861, the Pony Express had closed down. It had indeed played a glorious, if brief, part in American history and inspired many a tale about the heroics of its riders. Other black men participated in that heyday of the Pony Express. James Francis, William Robinson, John Hall, and a famous Indian scout named Jim Beckwourth were all a part of those "glory days."

George Monroe went on to become a famous stagecoach driver some years later. In fact, in 1879 he was picked to drive President Ulysses S. Grant along the dangerous curves of the Wanona Trail into the Yosemite Valley. George did such a good job that a meadow, called "Monroe Meadows," was named after him in Yosemite Valley.

"So you see, Sundown, that's how the West eventually got its mail service. Those Pony Express riders were the very best and bravest our nation had to offer. All of us owe a lot to the pioneer spirit of those men of the Pony Express."

When the Old Cowboy talked about the black pioneers, his feelings of pride always soared. He knew they threw caution to the wind and trusted themselves to pull through adversity, so that they might blaze new trails—to opportunity and freedom!

BIBLIOGRAPHY

Bonner, T. D. *The Life and Adventures of James P. Beckwourth.* New York: Arno Press, 1969.

Durham, Philip and Jones, Everett L. *The Adventures of the Negro Cowboys.* New York: Dodd Mead, 1960.

Durham, Philip, and Jones, Everett L. *The Negro Cowboys.* New York: Dodd Mead, 1965.

Feldon, Howard. *Edward Rose, Negro Trailblazer.* New York: Dodd Mead, 1966.

Goode, Kenneth G. *California's Black Pioneers.* Santa Barbara, CA: McNally & Loftin, 1974.

Katz, William Loren. *Black Indians: A Hidden Heritage*. Seattle, WA: Ethrac Publications, 1986.

Katz, William Loren. *The Black West*. New York: Doubleday/Anchor, 1987.

Katz, William Loren. *Eyewitness: The Negro in American History*. New York: Putnam, 1967.

Leckie, William H. *The Military Conquest of the Southern Plains*. University of Oklahoma Press, 1963.

Lee, Irvin. *Negro Medal of Honor*. New York: Dodd Mead, 1967.

Millis, Walter. *The Martial Spirit*. Boston: Little Brown, 1931.

Stewart, Paul W., and Ponce, Yvonne Wallace. *Black Cowboys*. Broomfield, CO.: Phillips Publishing, 1986.